ON FOOT ON
HIGH WEALD

18 medium and long walks in the Weald of Sussex and Kent

BEN PERKINS

S.B. Publications

By the same author

South Downs: Walks for Motorists
Pub Walks in the South Downs
Village Walks in East Sussex
Waterside Walks in Sussex
Sussex Border Path: Guide and Map Pack
On Foot on the East Sussex Downs
On Foot on the West Sussex Downs
Classic Walks in Sussex

Contributed walks to:

Walkers Britain and Walkers Britain 2
AA Book of Village Walks
Exploring Britain's Long Distance Paths
AA Book of Family Walks

First published in 2003 by S.B. Publications
19 Grove Road, Seaford, East Sussex BN25 1TP
Tel: 01323 893498 Fax: 01323 893860
E-mail: sbpublications@tiscali.co.uk

ISBN 1-85770-270-0

Designed and Typeset by EH Graphics, East Sussex (01273) 515527
Printed by Pageturn Ltd, East Sussex, BN3 7EG. Tel: (01273) 821500

Front Cover photo: View across the Eden Valley from path between points 6 and 7, walk 3.
Back Cover photo: View towards Friends' Clump from path between points 2 and 3, walk 5
Title Page photo: Hairpin loop in the River Medway between points 11 and 12, walk 8.

CONTENTS

INTRODUCTION

Most visitors, when seeking out the best walking in the southeast corner of England, head for the South Downs or the parallel chalk ridge of the North Downs. But in between the two, the High Weald, though much less well known, offers a landscape of great beauty and variety. In a wide swathe across the northern part of Mid and East Sussex and straddling the border with Kent, an outcrop of sandstone forms two long broken ridges which extend eastwards from St.Leonard's Forest, near Horsham to reach the sea to the east of Hastings. The designated High Weald Area of Outstanding Natural Beauty, embraces the whole of this ridge as well as the upper valleys of the Medway and the Eastern Rother which penetrate deeply into the higher ground.

In 1994 the Countryside Commission published a landscape assessment of the High Weald, dividing it into nine 'character areas' which I have used to distribute and place the eighteen walks in this book. The walks vary in length from 5 to 11 miles. Though many of them can be completed as a brisk half day hike they are designed to occupy a leisurely full day out, with plenty of time to linger and enjoy the sights along the way and drop in on the pubs or tea rooms which are passed on many of the circuits. Several of the walks pass close to historical sites such as Penshurst Place (Walk 3), Bodiam Castle (Walk 13) or Battle Abbey (Walk 15).

The starting points of the majority of the walks are accessible using public transport though bus services are scanty and often confined to weekdays. I have included a brief outline of the relevant bus and train services with each walk and all but two of the walks start and finish at public car parks.

This is a thinly populated area and some of the rights of way are little used. Signing and waymarking is patchy and the paths are not always maintained to a high standard though all of them were unobstructed and practicable when I checked the walks during the summer of 2002. However, particularly in late summer, some of the less frequented paths may become overgrown and I would recommend taking a stout stick to beat down any encroaching brambles or nettles.

The route descriptions are comprehensive and detailed but the accompanying sketch maps are little more than a simple outline. They cannot be used to follow the walk with any accuracy and are no help at all should you stray from the described route. I would, therefore, strongly recommend always having the relevant Ordnance Survey Explorer map to hand before setting out.

For me, the preparation of this book has been something of a journey of discovery, penetrating deeply into this rich and varied landscape, with something new and often surprising round almost every turn in the path. I hope you will enjoy a similar experience.

LOCATION OF WALKS

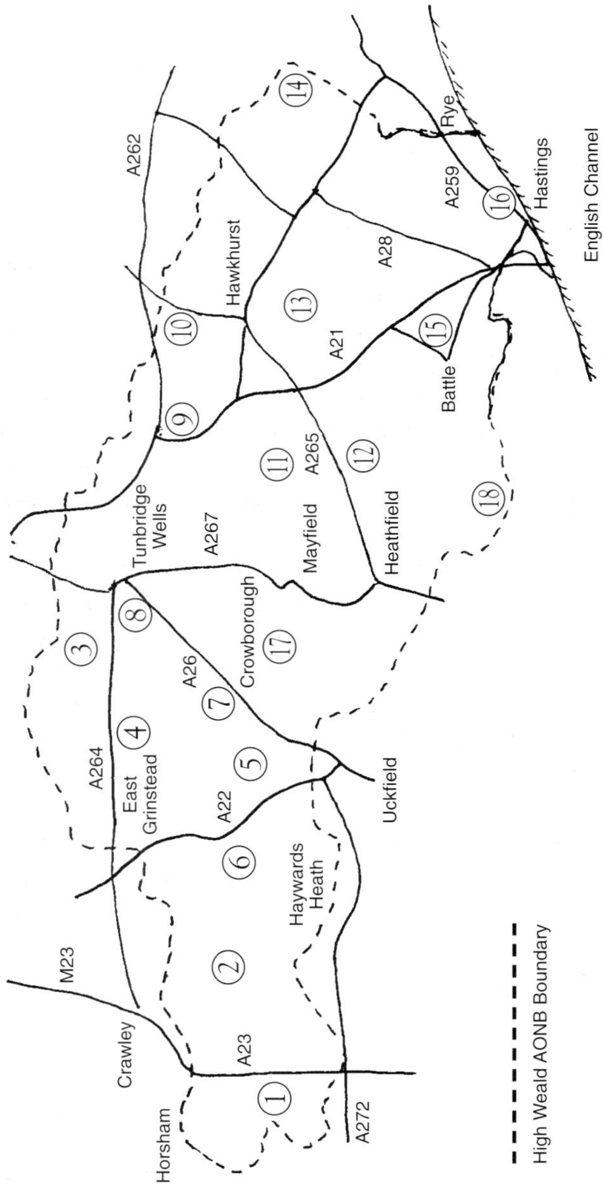

Walk 1

SLAUGHAM AND WARNINGLID

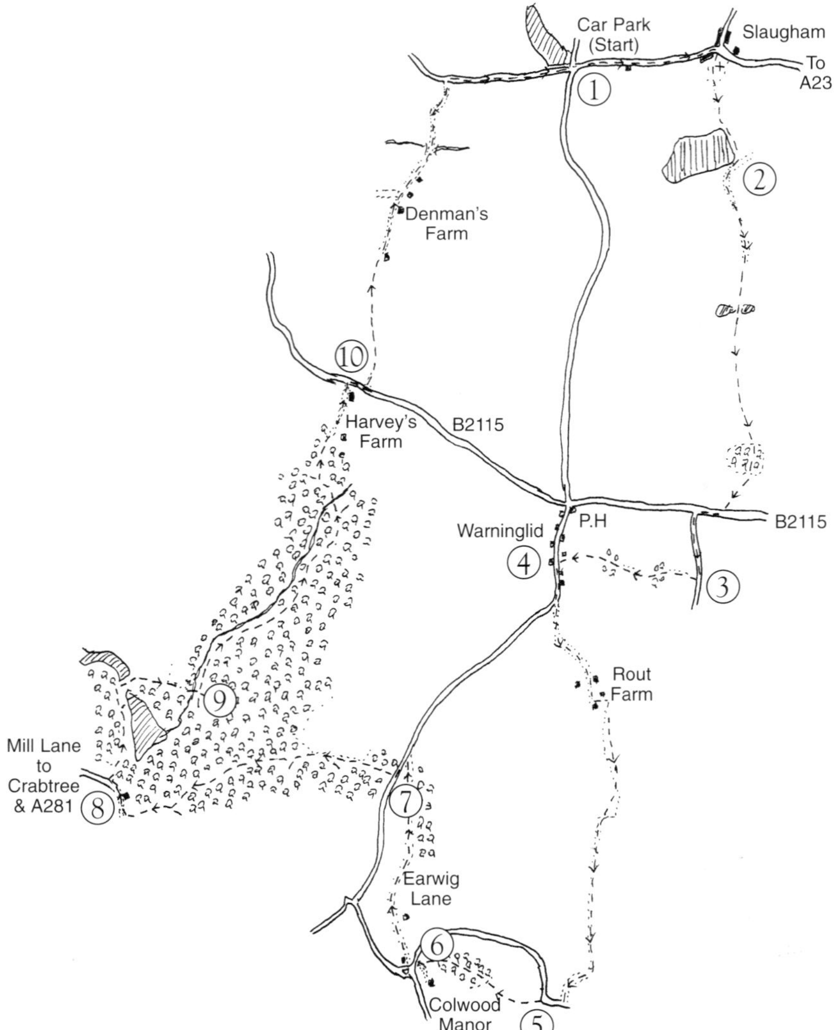

Walk 1

SLAUGHAM AND WARNINGLID

Distance:	$8^3/_4$ miles
Route:	Furnace Pond (west of Slaugham) - Slaugham - High Weald Landscape Trail - Warninglid - Rout Farm - Colwood Park - Colwood Manor - Earwig Lane - Steep Wood - Minepits Wood - Harvey's Farm - Furnace Pond.
Map:	OS Explorer 134: Crawley and Horsham.
Start/Parking:	Access from the A23 north of Bolney, signposted to Slaugham. Park in the small car parking area immediately north of the cross roads and next to Furnace Pond at GR 250280.
Public Transport:	Bus to Crabtree and walk east (1/2 mile) along Mill Lane to join the walk at point 8.
Conditions:	Mostly along well signed and used field and woodland paths. Muddy in places.
Refreshments:	Pub at Warninglid, a short distance off the route from point 4.

The Western High Weald is characterised by extensive woodland, a pleasant mix of broad-leaved trees, patches of dense conifer plantation and, in places, profuse undergrowth of invasive rhododendron as well as more open areas of heathland where bracken is peppered with young larch and silver birch. Although much of the walk passes through these woods you will, for the first two miles, be heading south across a more open ridge with superb views southwards to the South Downs. The walk starts from a pond at the source of the River Ouse and you will come across several similar secluded lakes and ponds which were originally dammed in medieval times to form hammer ponds, providing a steady flow of water to power the bellows used in the once-flourishing iron industry.

THE WALK

From the cross roads next to the car parking area **(1),** *follow the lane eastwards, signposted to Slaugham and Staplefield. After almost half a mile, turn right into Slaugham churchyard.*

Slaugham Church has a 13th century tower with a so-called 'Sussex cap' and contains the tomb of Richard Covert of nearby Slaugham Place, now a ruin. He died in 1579 and his monument represents him, kneeling, with his two wives and fourteen children. The village is no more than a small cluster of dwellings and a restaurant-type pub, not geared for thirsty walkers as you cannot buy a drink without also purchasing food!

Skirt to the right of the church and continue in the same direction through the churchyard and on along the right edge of an area planted with young trees. A path skirts to the left of a large pond, the site of major recent earthworks, designed to secure the dam at the head of the pond. At the far end of this dam **(2),** *turn right along an unmade track, shortly ignoring a signed path to the right. The track acquires a metalled surface for a while and then becomes an attractive green lane before continuing as a headland path along a left field edge.*

Furnace pond next to start

Pond between points 1 and 2.

In the field corner, go over a stile on the right and head half right across pasture to find the next stile. Go forward between two ponds. Confusingly, neither the ponds, nor a new house over to your right are yet marked on OS maps. A trodden path carries on across pasture, then climbs gently through a wood and on across a field, diverging gradually from a fence on the left, to join the B2115 road (Cuckfield Lane).

Turn right and, after a little over 100 yards, go left along Colwood Lane. After another 300 yards **(3)**, *go over a stile beside a gate to follow another well established path along a right field edge. After 100 yards or so, fork right through an iron kissing gate, walk through a wood to a similar gate and along the right edge of the field beyond. The path passes through another thicket and continues beside a field, past allotments and between houses to join a lane at Warninglid* **(4)**.

The village comprises a prosperous mix of old and new houses, many constructed in the local vernacular brick with hung tiles. The Half Moon, a good pub for walkers, is a short distance along the road to the right. Return the same way.

To continue the walk turn left at point 4, heading south out of the village. Where the road curves round to the right, go ahead along the gravel drive to Rout Farm. At the farm, after a little over a quarter of a mile, follow bridleway signs left for 60 yards then right through a blue gate and on to the next bridle gate, in sight, keeping fairly close to the fence on your right.

From this relatively high vantage point you have a fine panoramic view of the Downs ahead of you, close enough to pick out, from left to right, the bare

Slaugham Church.

promontory of Wolstonbury Hill with the wooded Newtimber Hill behind it, the tree clump next to the Devil's Dyke Hotel, the radio masts on Truleigh Hill, the Adur gap and the Downs escarpment rising westwards to the battered remains of Chanctonbury Ring, still just about recognisable.

Continue beside the fence on your right until you can go right through a gate in this fence and resume your previous direction, now with the fence on your left. In the field corner, go ahead through another bridle gate and ahead along an enclosed path. Where this grassy path ends, go right along a drive, following it as it curves round to the left past several houses and out to join a road.

Turn right and, after a few yards, where the lane bends away to the right **(5),** *go ahead along a rough track. After 10 yards only, fork left along a narrow path which descends to cross a culvert and stile before climbing along a wide grass strip with a wood to your right and a high fence to the left. In the field corner, go through a gap and uphill along a left field edge. Shortly, where the fence on your left turns away to the left, go ahead across grass without change in direction to enter a wood over a stile beside a gate. Follow a right hand fence through the wood to join a drive where you should turn right out to a lane at a junction* **(6).**

Go forward along the road opposite for 10 yards only before going right along the drive to a house called Beehouses which narrows to an enclosed path. Follow this ancient trackway (Earwig Lane) for half a mile through to another lane. Turn left and, after a little over 100 yards **(7),** *go right along a narrow signed path which starts through a wooden gate, burrows through a thicket and joins a bridleway coming in from behind on the left. Where footpath and bridleway divide again, keep right (in effect straight on) along the signed footpath. It passes through thick woodland at first, and then crosses a more open area of bracken and scattered trees. After about a quarter of a mile, the bridleway is rejoined, once again coming in from behind on the left.*

Ignore two tracks going off to the right, keeping along the main bridleway track as it skirts to the left of a pond. Leave the wood through a gate, bear right up to a second gate and turn right along a gravel track, passing, on your right, a delightful cottage with a roof of Horsham stone.

Where the drive becomes a lane **(8),** *turn sharply back to the right along a wide track. After 400 yards the path bears right across a dam between two large lakes.*

The high perimeter fence on your left surrounds Leonardslee Gardens. Although inaccessible from the path, the Gardens are open to the public from April to October and are probably at their best in the spring when Magnolias, Camellias, Azalea and Rhododendron provide colourful displays. As an added novelty, wallabies roam semi-wild in part of the estate. The entrance is from the A281 road.

The path continues through the wood and then within the wood edge with a large open field to your left before plunging down through the trees once more. Cross a stream using a bridge made from two stone slabs **(9).** *Just beyond the stream, at a fingerpost, turn left along the valley with the stream meandering through a swampy area to your left.*

After more than half a mile, a few yards after passing a path coming in through a swing gate from your right, which you should ignore, turn left between staggered railings along a narrow, descending, water-eroded path, A wooden causeway takes you across a swampy area, after which the path climbs fairly steeply.

Go straight over an oblique unsigned crossing path, still climbing between banks. After less than 100 yards, at a signed path junction, turn right, gaining more height. Where five paths converge, take the third exit in roundabout terms (virtually straight ahead). Beyond a stile the path joins an access drive which continues out to the B2115 road **(10).**

Turn right and, after less than 100 yards, go left along a signed bridleway, fenced between two fields, through a wood and then along a left field edge, tiresomely enclosed and soggy underfoot in places. Beyond a cottage, the bridleway joins and follows a metalled access drive for half a mile out to a road. Turn right and follow the road for another 600 yards back to the start.

Warninglid.

Walk 2

WEST HOATHLY AND SELSFIELD COMMON

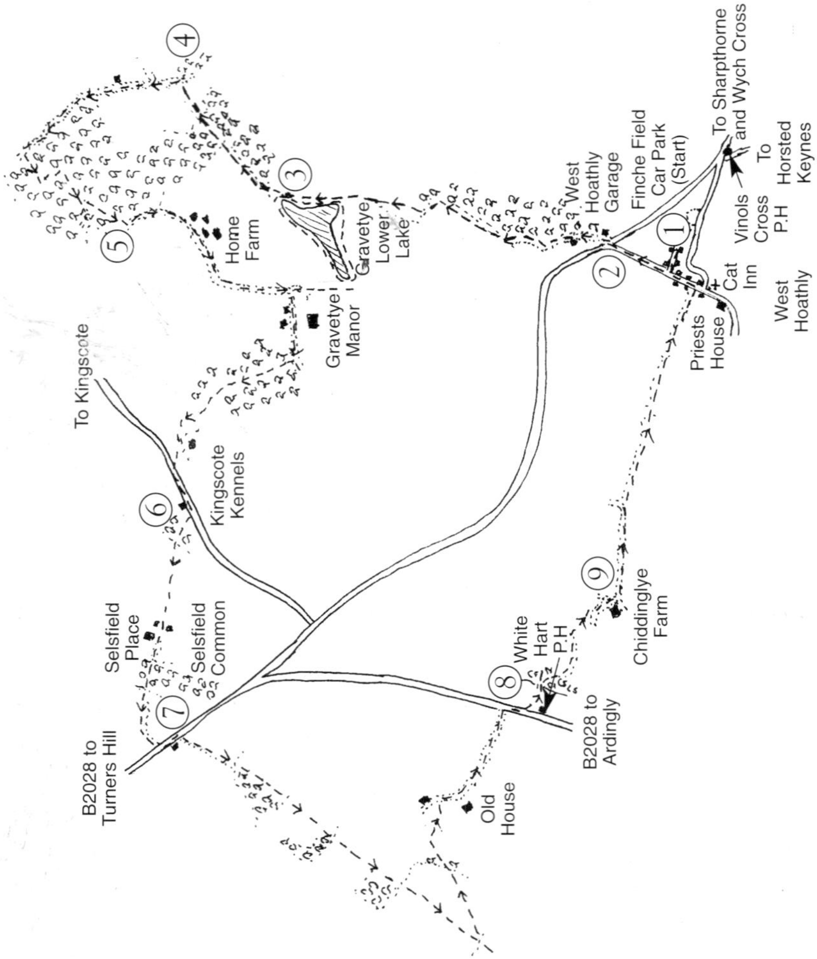

Walk 2

WEST HOATHLY AND SELSFIELD COMMON

Distance:	$6^1/_4$ miles
Route:	West Hoathly - Gravetye Lower Lake - Bushy Wood - High Weald Landscape Trail - Gravetye Manor - Selsfield Common - Old House - Chiddinglye Farm - West Hoathly.
Map:	OS Explorer 135: Ashdown Forest.
Start/Parking:	From West Hoathly, accessible eastwards from the B2028 Haywards Heath-to-Turners Hill road. Park in the Finche Field car park and picnic area, marked with a 'P' on the Explorer map to the north of the road about 250 yards east of the church and the Cat Inn (GR 366326).
Public Transport:	Weekday bus service to West Hoathly from Haywards Heath or Crawley.
Conditions:	A moderately up-and-down walk, much of it on sandy woodland paths or tracks.
Refreshments:	Pubs at West Hoathly and at point 8, about two thirds of the way round the walk.

Much of the earlier part of this walk explores an area of dense woodland to the north of West Hoathly, most of it managed by the Forestry Commission. A short detour offers a circuit of a quietly secluded lake, tucked deeply down in a wooded valley. A steady climb then takes you up to Selsfield Common, an attractive National Trust area of mixed heath and woodland. On the return route, an open field path walk across high ground with fine views southwards towards the Sussex Downs provides a pleasant contrast with the thick woodland of the outward journey.

Brick and tile-hung cottages, West Hoathly.

THE WALK

From the far end of the car park **(1),** *follow a tarmac path which passes a picnic area, running parallel to the road in a defile to your left.*

A topograph beside the path, at this high point, over 600 feet above sea level, indicates the direction of various places. Views are limited but, on a clear day, the South Downs are visible over a hedge to the south.

Ignoring steps down to the road on your left, follow the path to join the end of a cul-de-sac. Follow this estate road out to a T-junction with another road and turn right. At a junction with another busy road **(2),** *go ahead along the access to West Hoathly Garage, passing to the left of the garage buildings and continuing along a metalled drive which becomes a hedged path. Ignoring a path which forks left over a stile, carry on downhill between high wooded banks. After a few yards, where once again you have choice of signed paths, keep left and, shortly, fork left again to a stile and continue downhill, keeping to the right field edge.*

Over to your left, half hidden by trees, the manor of Gravetye comes into view. Built in 1598, it was once the seat of the Infield family, Sussex ironmasters. It is now a country hotel.

Follow the field edge as it turns squarely round to the left and, after less than 100 yards, go right along a dirt track which takes you through a belt of woodland. Head out across the next field, walking parallel to and then gradually converging on the left lower field edge. From the far left field corner, go ahead along a sunken track. It is boggy in places but there is an alternative path for part of the way on the top of the bank to the right **(3).**

West Hoathly Church.

Gravetye Lake.

A gate on the left of the track provides access, during the summer months only, to Gravetye Lower Lake, one of the sources of the River Medway. It is a delightful spot and a complete circuit of the lake will add only half a mile to the walk.

Resuming your progress from point 3 along the sunken track, drop down and emerge into the open through a gate or the stile beside it. Now turn right along the right edge of two fields with thick woodland on your right. In the second field corner, go through an iron kissing gate, straight ahead through a wood and on in the same direction across a field to a stile providing access to a metalled drive **(4).** *Turn left along this drive and, at a junction with another drive, go straight ahead, joining the waymarked High Weald Landscape Trail which you will be following for the next mile or so.*

Ignore the first signed route off to the left (a permissive bridleway) and, after another 300 yards, turn left along a signed footpath which passes between low wooden posts and continues through woodland. After about 150 yards, go left along a crossing path, descend to cross a stream and, after a few more yards, fork right uphill, signed to Vowels Car Park. After 10 yards only, where the path divides, keep left, climbing steadily through the wood.

At a T-junction **(5),** *turn left along a solidly based track. Shortly, join and go ahead along a roughly metalled drive which passes to the right of the complex of*

Gravetye Manor.

buildings at Home Farm. Join and turn left along the drive to Gravetye Manor. At the main gateway to the manor, turn right along a back drive, signed as a private road but also as a bridal (sic!) and footpath.

From here, if day and time are right, you can break off the walk for a tour of Gravetye Manor gardens, using a waymarked circular route, open only on Tuesdays and Fridays between 10 and 5. The gardens were laid out by William Robinson, one of the pioneers of the 'natural' garden.

Our walk follows the drive past some outbuildings, with Gravetye Manor and garden down the slope to your left. After about 250 yards, turn right along a signed footpath which tunnels up through a thicket, skirts to the right of a house and garden and continues to join a drive where you should bear right for a few yards out to a road and turn left.

Walk beside this busy road with some care until, just past the entrance to Kingscote Kennels **(6),** *you can fork right through a gate to follow a clear track, through woodland at first, then across high open ground.*

For the last mile or so you have been gradually gaining height and you are now rewarded with a fine, though intermittent, view northwards across the valley of the River Eden to the distant North Downs.

Pass between the outbuildings and to the left of the big house at Selsfield Place and ahead on a grassy strip between fences. Beyond a wicket gate, go forward across the National Trust area of Selsfield Common, a pleasant mix of heath and thin woodland. At a signed path junction, fork right down shallow steps and, after a few yards, ignoring a stiled path to the right, walk out to the edge of the common where there is a well placed seat with a view, marred only by a tangle of electricity wires in the foreground. Go ahead along a field edge, following the left hand hedge round to the left and out to join the B2028 road. Turn left beside this busy road, walking on the narrow right hand verge. After less than 200 yards **(7),** *turn right through a gap in the hedge and forward along a right field edge. Beyond a stile in the field corner, head straight out on a stiled and signed route across three fields, skirting to the left of two blocks of woodland.*

In the fourth field, your official route goes straight ahead until, just short of a stile at the far end of the field, it doubles back to the left, staying within the same field and running roughly parallel to power lines to reach a stile. You may be forgiven by the farmer, however if, from the start of this fourth field, you simply follow a short cut round the left edge to the stile, in sight over to your left, thus avoiding an acute dog-leg along cross-field paths.

Whichever route you choose, once over the stile, drop obliquely down a grassy bank shaded by a row of fine mature trees and cross a meadow to go through a wide gateway (not the swing gate a few yards to the right of this gate). Go forward for a few yards to a stile beside a gate and then bear half right along a right field edge to another pair of stiles sandwiching a sleeper bridge. Continue for a few yards to another stile. A path climbs sharply, aided by steps and hand rail and continues to join a drive. Turn right to follow this pleasant ornamental drive out between a pair of ponds and on to rejoin the B2028 road **(8).** *Turn right.*

The path between points 7 and 8.

Ornamental lake beside the drive from Old House, approaching point 8.

In sight, a little way along the road is the White Hart Inn, housed in an attractive half-timbered building. It proclaims itself as a 14th Century Inn with a 16th Century restaurant.

To complete the walk, a few yards short of the pub, turn left over a step in a low brick wall. The path drops down into a shallow valley. Cross a culverted stream and immediately turn right on a path through thick woodland. Cross a plank bridge, go over a stile and bear right across pasture, contouring along near the foot of a grassy slope, rising to your left, until you can go right over a stile in an iron fence and follow a well trodden path through woodland to a kissing gate and forward along a metalled drive. At a three-armed fingerpost, next to Chiddinglye Farm **(9),** *where a number of drives and tracks meet, turn left along the main concrete drive from the farm. If you have a compass you should now be heading due east. Where the drive turns squarely away to the left, go ahead on a headland track along a left field edge with the spire of West Hoathly church intermittently in your sights ahead. The path takes a direct route back to reach the road at West Hoathly, opposite the Cat Inn.*

The church, across the road to the right, is much restored, but has a fine shingled spire. A few yards along the lane which starts to the right of the church is the half-timbered 15th Century Priest's House. The house and garden are open between March and October on weekdays between 11 and 5 and on Sunday afternoons between 2 and 5.

To complete the walk, turn left on reaching the road and after about 150 yards, go right along Sandy Lane, retracing your outgoing route to the start.

Cat Inn, West Hoathly

Walk 3

PENSHURST, CHIDDINGSTONE AND HEVER

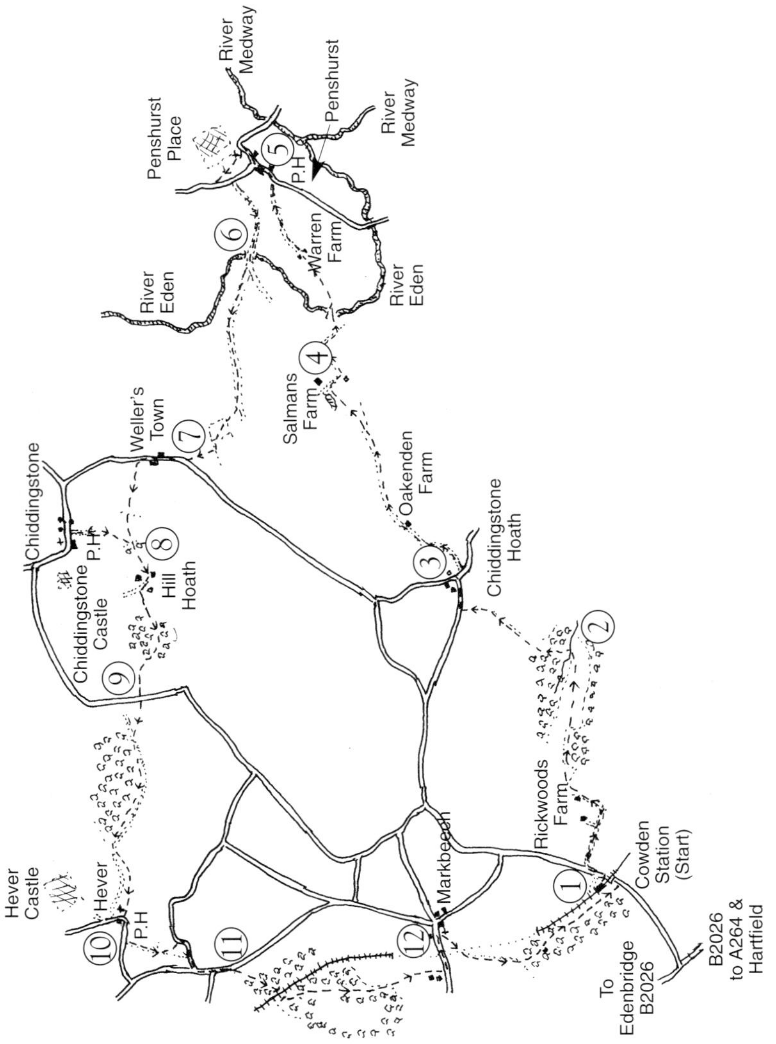

Walk 3

PENSHURST, CHIDDINGSTONE AND HEVER

Distance:	11 miles
Route:	Cowden Station - Rickwoods Farm - Chiddingstone Hoath - Penshurst - Weller's Town - Chiddingstone - Hever - Markbeech - Cowden Station.
Map:	OS Explorer 147: Sevenoaks and Tonbridge
Start/Parking:	From Cowden Station. Easiest access is from the B2026 Hartfield-to-Edenbridge road about $1^1/_2$ miles north of its junction with the A264 East Grinstead-to-Tunbridge Wells road. (GR 476417)
Public Transport:	Train to Cowden (weekdays only) on the Oxted-to-Uckfield line.
Conditions:	Good walking mostly along well defined paths and tracks. Gently undulating without serious hills.
Refreshments:	Pubs at Penshurst, Chiddingstone, Hever and Markbeech. Tea rooms at Penshurst and Chiddingstone.

A glance at the Explorer map shows clearly the concentrated patchwork of woodland on the southern slopes of the Eden valley explored on this substantial and varied walk. After picking a fairly intricate route through this beautiful landscape, our walk descends into the wide valley where the Medway and the Eden, its main tributary, join to the south of Penshurst. The return journey passes close to no less than three stately homes, all open to the public and well worth a visit, though possibly on separate occasions since the walk itself will occupy the best part of a full day out.

Penshurst Place originated in the 14th century but has been much extended since that time, and is surrounded by landscaped parkland. **Hever Castle** is more of a fortified manor than a castle, built in1453 as the home of the Bullen family. Anne Bullen (Boleyn) spent her childhood there. In the last century William Waldorf Astor, the American millionaire, renovated the building and created an Italian Garden and a 40-acre lake. Like Hever, **Chiddingstone Castle** is not really a castle at all, but a 17th century house with sandstone castellated trimmings in Gothic revival style.

THE WALK

From Cowden Station **(1)** *follow the station approach road out to a junction and turn left. After 150 yards go right along a metalled access drive. About 100 yards after passing the access to Rickwood's Farm on your left, go left along a gravel drive. About 50 yards short of a house, go right over a stile and resume your previous direction, skirting closely to the right of the house and garden before veering half right past a power pole to a stile, in sight. Veer half right across the next field, past a concrete water trough and a waypost, from which your next stile is in view. A clear path continues within the left lower edge of sloping woodland.*

Leave the wood over a stile and go ahead contouring along a gently sloping grassy hillside between two areas of woodland. About 150 yards short of the end of this long thin field, bear left down to a stile into woodland. Cross a stream **(2)** *and turn left.*

South of Chiddingstone Hoath.

'Leicester Square', Penshurst.

After a few yards, fork right with the main path which climbs steadily up through the wood. At the top of this steep rise, go ahead on a path joining from behind on the right, to a stile and on along a right field edge, climbing gently.

In the field corner, follow the field edge round to the left. Ignore a gate on the right, but after five more yards, go right over a stile into woodland. Walk through a wood and then bear round to the right, following a high right-hand hedge out to a lane. Turn right into Chiddingstone Hoath **(3).**

Chiddingstone Hoath is a modest settlement, little more than a cluster of cottages, some old, facing on to a small triangular village green. In the centre of the green is a large sandstone boulder with the carved inscription 'The Hoath MM'.

Follow the main road round to the right, signposted to Penshurst, and after a few yards, go left along a metalled access drive. At Oakenden Farm, follow the track ahead and, shortly, continue ahead, passing to the right of a double garage, now on a narrower path which leads out into a field. Drop down along the left edge of two fields. Soon after encircling to the right of a pond, go over a stile in the field corner and forward through a wood. Shortly bear right for 15 yards, then, at a waypost, left over a short plank bridge, through trees to a stile and on along the left edge of two fields. In the second field cross a stile and follow a signed path diversion left to a swing gate

Penshursh Churchyard.

and on beside a fence where Penshurst Place comes into view directly ahead. Go through two more swing gates with steps between them, then right along a wide grassy strip. Join a drive next to Salman's Farm **(4)**, *a converted oast over to the left, go forward for 20 yards, then right between low posts and along another wide fenced path. After 100 yards, go left over a stile and ahead along the left edge of two fields. In the second field corner follow the field edge round to the right until, after about 150 yards, you can go left over a stile. Cross the River Eden, go forward to a stile and on along a left field edge. Go past the buildings at Warren Farm and follow the farm access drive ahead for a quarter of a mile out to the B2188 road. Turn left into Penshurst, passing the old village Smithy, now a shop and garage. At the road junction in the centre of the village* **(5)**, *go ahead passing the Leicester Arms on your right. Shortly go left into Penshurst churchyard.*

The lovely little courtyard in front of the church entrance, surrounded by tile-hung and timber-framed Tudor cottages, is Leicester Square, named after the Earl of Leicester, one of the courtiers of Elizabeth I. The entrance to Penshurst church tunnels beneath one of these cottages, supported by wooden props.

Skirt to the left of the 19th century sandstone church, notable as the burial place of the Sidneys of Penshurst Place, go through a squeeze stile and head out half left across parkland to join a road. Turn left and, after about 100 yards, go right along the metalled access drive to Salman's Farm. About 70 yards after crossing the River Eden **(6),** *fork right along an unmade track, climbing gently.*

You are now following part of the Eden Valley Walk, a 15-mile waymarked route linking Edenbridge with Tonbridge. The River Eden winds along the foot of the slope to your right for a while as a view opens up northward towards the rag stone ridge around Ide Hill and Toy's Hill.

After over half a mile, go right over a stile and head out half left down across pasture to cross a stile and footbridge in the bottom field corner. Resume your previous direction diagonally across a field of vines where a path has been left between the plants. In the far corner, go ahead through a gap in a hedge, forward for 30 yards along a right field edge and then right across a culvert and ahead on a preserved grass strip between two large fields out to join a lane **(7).**

Turn right through the tiny settlement of Weller's Town, little more than a couple of rows of cottages. Follow the lane down and across a stream and, after a few more yards, turn left through a gate and follow a, normally well-defined, path across two fields.

On the far side of the second field, just short of a stile into a wood **(8),** *you have a choice. If you would prefer to omit the detour to Chiddingstone, a quarter of a mile*

View across the Eden Valley from path between points 6 and 7.

each way, go ahead over the stile. To visit Chiddingstone, turn sharply right on another cross-field path and on along an enclosed path out to Chiddingstone village street. The village centre and the church are now a few yards away to the left.

The half-timbered houses lining the village street, as well as the Castle Inn and the village shop, are owned by the National Trust. The Chiding Stone, from which the village gets its name, is accessible along a signposted path from the village street. It was apparently used, in ancient times, as a seat of judgement, though not on this site.

Retrace your steps to point 8, cross the stile and go ahead between two small ponds. Go forward across an area of neglected pasture and patchy scrub to a stile and on to join a track. Follow this track between the buildings and round to the right at Hill Hoath. At a junction turn left along another roughly metalled drive, signed as a private road. Where it ends, go ahead on a path which soon burrows dramatically between high sandstone banks. A few yards beyond the point where the path leaves the wood, fork right to a stile and then bear left through more open coppiced woodland, descending to a stream and on between fences out to a lane **(9).**

Follow a clear, well trodden path, opposite. Cross a drive to a gate. From here, walk parallel and to the right of the drive at first, then, after crossing the drive on a high footbridge, to the left of the drive, on a segregated path which takes you out to a road through Hever churchyard **(10).**

The entrance to Hever Castle is now a few yards along the road to the right but, to continue the walk, turn left and follow the road round to the right, leaving the King Henry VIII Inn on your right. After about 200 yards, opposite the village hall on your right, go left over a stile and ahead along a field edge to another stile. In the next field, soon veer slightly left across the grass to join a lane over a stile beside a gate in the far left field corner.

Turn right along the road and, at a road junction, turn left, signposted to Markbeech and Cowden. Ignore a turning to the right, signed to Hever Station, and, after another 100 yards or so **(11),** *fork right along a fenced path. Soon after passing under the railway, fork left up rudimentary steps and continue on a path which heads generally southwards through woodland.*

Although labelled Oak Wood on the map, there are now few oak trees remaining, though there has been much replanting, mostly beech.

At the far end of the wood, fork left along a fenced path which eventually skirts to the left of buildings at Bramsell's Farm and brings you to a lane. Turn left beside a road into Markbeech **(12).**

Markbeech is a modest settlement though it does boast a church and a conveniently placed pub, the Kentish Horse.

Just short of the church, and within sight of the pub, turn right, hugging the right edge of the churchyard until, after a few yards you can leave it over a stile in the churchyard boundary hedge. Cross a drive and head out half left across pasture. Skirt to the right of a small sewage treatment works and drop downhill along the left edge of a large field until you can sidestep left over a stile and resume your previous direction downhill along a right field edge. In the field corner, cross a culvert and go forward along a clear woodland path, ignoring stiles on the right and left.

You will soon pass a small fairytale cottage, with a tall red brick chimney and tile-hung walls, hidden deep in the wood.

From the cottage, go ahead along a more substantial track. After a few yards, where this track goes off to the right, go ahead, once more on a woodland path. Ignore a path which drops away to your right across a footbridge. At another path junction, go ahead through a swing gate and along a lovely wooded valley to join a road. Turn left beneath the railway and left again, to Cowden Station.

OPENING TIMES

Penshurst Place: April-Sept, daily except Monday, 1 to 5.30 (Tel: 01892 870307)

Chiddingstone Castle: during the summer, Tuesday to Sunday (Tel: 01892 870347).

Hever Castle: open all year, Mon-Fri 9 to 5, Sat and Sun, 10 to 5 (Tel: 01732 865224).

The Chiddingstone, Chiddingstone.

Walk 4

HOLTYE AND HARTFIELD

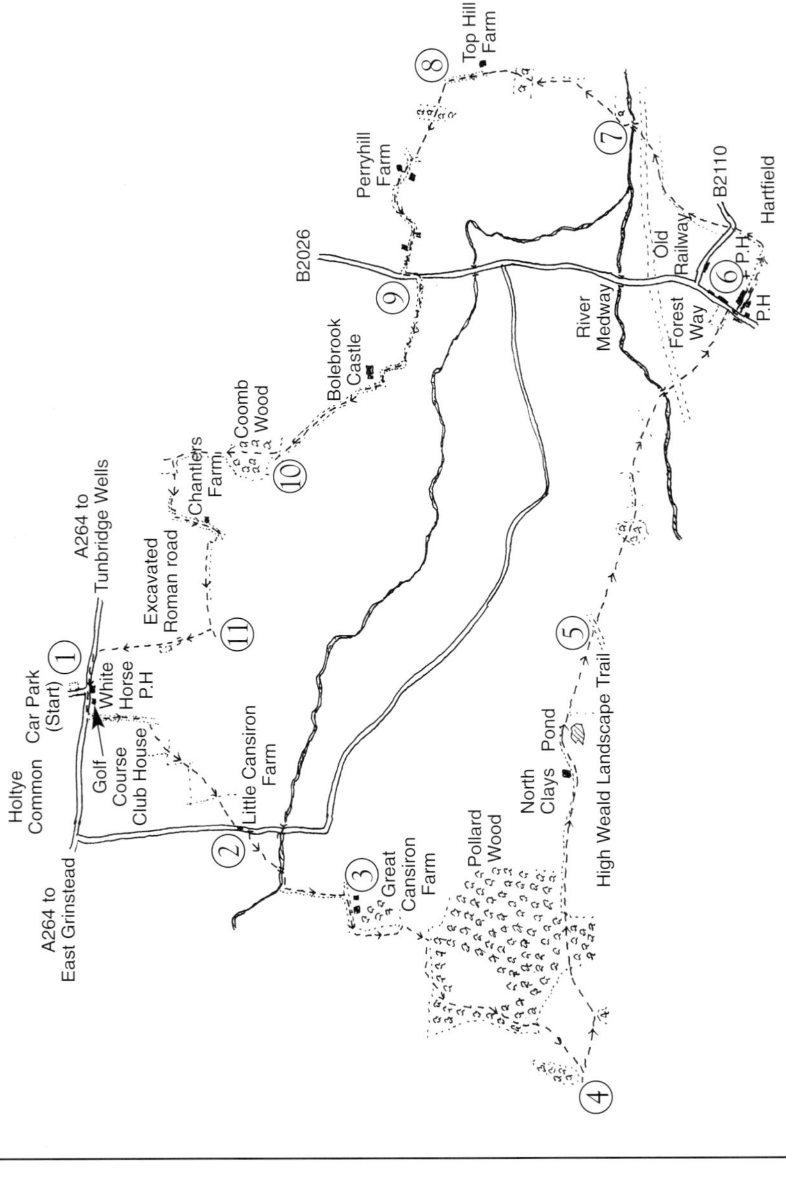

Walk 4

HOLTYE AND HARTFIELD

Distance:	9 miles
Route:	Holtye Common - Great Cansiron Farm - Pollard Wood - North Clays - Hartfield - Top Hill Farm - Perryhill Farm - Bolebrook Castle - Coomb Wood - Chantlers Farm - Holtye Common.
Map:	OS Explorer 135: Ashdown Forest.
Start/Parking:	From Holtye on the A264 East Grinstead-to-Tunbridge Wells road about five miles east of East Grinstead. Park in the car park a few yards along the road which heads north from the A264 opposite the White Horse pub. (GR 459393)
Public Transport:	Occasional weekday bus from East Grinstead or Tunbridge Wells
Conditions:	An undulating walk, mainly on good field and woodland paths. Several hills, none long or steep. May be muddy underfoot in places.
Refreshments:	White Horse pub at Holtye. Pubs and tea rooms at Hartfield.

Rising to the south of East Grinstead, the River Medway flows eastwards for several miles before turning northwards towards Tonbridge. This walk starts on a ridge to the north of the main river valley, descending to cross a minor tributary stream before climbing again to a ridge overlooking the main Medway valley (point 4) offering a fine panoramic view southwards to the heights of Ashdown Forest.

Continuing eastwards along the ridge, it then drops down, crossing the Medway to reach the attractive village of Hartfield, at its best out of season when the hordes of Winnie-the-Pooh fans who flock to the village and the nearby Poohs(sticks) Bridge have gone home. The return route re-crosses the Medway and climbs again, then undulating across two minor streams and passing through Coomb Wood beyond point 10, a superb spot for bluebells in the spring.

THE WALK

From the car park ***(1)*** *return to the A264 and turn right in the East Grinstead direction. After about 100 yards turn left along a roughly metalled drive. After another 250 yards go right over a stile and head half left across a horse paddock. Go over a stile in the far corner and forward along a right field edge. Shortly, where the field boundary turns squarely away to the right, veer slightly right down across a field to find a gap in the next hedge. Continue across the corner of the field beyond, go over a culverted stream in another wide hedge gap and head straight out across the next field. Pass immediately to the right of a tree clump and continue across the field to join a metalled drive* ***(2).*** *Turn left.*

After 100 yards or so, go right along a signed path which winds through trees before crossing a meadow to go over a substantial footbridge. Go right along the field edge. In the field corner you will come to another, more modest, bridge. Don't cross it. Instead, turn left to follow a right field edge up out of the valley. At the top ***(3)*** *turn right along a metalled drive past the farmhouse at Great Cansiron Farm.*

Across the valley to the right you can pick out the classical frontage of Hammerwood House, designed and built in 1790 by Benjamin Latrobe, the architect also responsible for the rebuilding of the Capitol in Washington DC.

Continue along the drive until, after about 200 yards, you can go left over a stile and sleeper bridge and forward with a wood on your left. At the corner of the wood, a useful fingerpost directs you to the right across a large field. On the other side of this field turn right along a wood edge until you are signed left into the wood. Follow the well waymarked path through Pollard Wood for almost half a mile.

Leave the wood over a stile and climb fairly steeply over humpy ground, soon veering slightly right and aiming, as soon as it is in view, for the left corner of a block of woodland and, just visible beyond it, a tall radio mast.

The climb is worth the effort as, from the corner of the wood, you are rewarded with a wide panoramic view to the south across the Medway valley and the heights of Ashdown Forest.

At the wood corner ***(4)*** *double sharply back to the left dropping down across a large area of pasture, soon aiming for the left end of a peninsula of woodland protruding into the field from the right. On reaching this wood veer half left across the field to a stile in the corner.*

You are now on part of the well-waymarked High Weald Landscape Trail which you will be following to Hartfield, making route finding easy.

Continue through a wood and on along the left edge of several fields. Skirt to the left of a pond and head out across the middle of the field beyond. Cross a drive **(5),** *go over a stile in a deer fence and head out half left across a field. Go over a stile beside a gate and maintain direction across the middle of the field beyond. In the far field corner you have a choice of two stiles. Go over the one on the left, through another deer fence, on within a wood, across a field to a gate and forward beside a left-hand hedge.*

Go over a stile by a gate and head out across two more fields, with the spire of Hartfield church, your next objective, soon in line ahead. Cross, in quick succession, the infant River Medway and the old railway, now the Forest Way, a long distance route for walkers and cyclists. A clear path continues between fields and out beside a recreation ground to the village street at Hartfield **(6).** *Turn right.*

Hartfield is an attractive village. Several cottages are clad in the locally characteristic white weatherboarding. There are two pubs and, further along the village street, tearooms and 'Pooh Corner', a shop dedicated to the sale of merchandise linked with Winnie the Pooh and other characters created by A. A. Milne who lived nearby.

After a few yards turn left along the access lane to the church, passing the Anchor Inn and subsequently the church on your left.

The lych gate into the churchyard tunnels beneath a delightful 16th Century half-timbered house and the church has a tall and elegant shingled spire.

Hartfield Churchyard.

The lane continues as a rough track. Where this track ends, turn left over a stile and follow the left edge of a meadow down to join the B2110. Go over the stile opposite and ahead, walking parallel to a fence, away to your left. Go over a stile in front of a massive tree stump and continue along the left edge of two fields. About half way along the second field, go left through a gate and diagonally across the next field.

Cross the old railway and the River Medway **(7)** *and follow a well-trodden path as it skirts to the left of a pond surrounded by trees. Go through a gap in a sparse hedge and climb steadily up across the middle of a field where a path is normally trodden out through any growing crop. Join and follow the right field edge up to the top field corner.*

This is a good point to pause to get your breath and look back for a fine view across Hartfield against a backdrop of the hills on the other side of the valley rising up to Ashdown Forest.

From the field corner a path continues through woodland and on along the right edge of a paddock. Beyond a large barn on your right, at a signed path junction, go forward along a track between fence and hedge. After about 250 yards **(8),** *go through two gates in quick succession and head out across a paddock, passing to the left of a fenced, tree-lined pond to enter woodland over a stile. Walk through the wood.*

On the other side of the wood is another excellent viewpoint, encompassing Hartfield and an extensive area of the undulating ground rising to the north of the Medway valley.

Drop down along a right field edge. In the field corner turn right along a track and, shortly, at a junction, turn right and follow a track and subsequently an access drive, between the buildings at Perryhill Farm and on for another quarter of a mile, past Bolebrook Farm and out to the B2026 **(9).** *Turn left and, after less than 100 yards, go right along the access drive to Bolebrook Castle.*

Bolebrook is more of an Elizabethan manor house than a castle but has a striking turreted gatehouse.

In front of the gateway to Bolebrook, go left with the drive and, after 50 yards, at a junction with another drive, go right, passing to the left of the gatehouse, half hidden from view on your right. Where the drive ends at a row of garages, go ahead along an unmade track. Shortly go forward along a wider track, joining from your left.

After about a quarter of a mile **(10),** *about 30 yards short of a gate, fork right on a narrower path which winds up through Coomb Wood, a truly delightful spot. From the top of the wood go forward along a meandering left field edge. When standing beneath power lines, don't be tempted by the stile ahead. Instead, go left with the field edge. In the field corner, go over a stile, immediately left over a second stile then right, now with a fence on your right. Walk round two sides of this field to a stile by a gate in the far corner leading out to a drive.*

Turn left. Beyond Chantlers Farm on the left the drive becomes a soft track, soon between banks. After about 100 yards, go right over a stile, forward through a gate, right to a second gate, then left beside a left hand hedge.

This is another fine vantage point for views northwards into Kent. The prominent spire in the middle distance is Cowden church.

In the field corner go over a stile and forward on a path which, rather unexpectedly winds down through an area of heathland, passing obliquely back under power lines. Continue down along the right edge of rough pasture until, after about 150 yards **(11)** *you can go right along a signed crossing path, through a wood and down along a right field edge. Cross a stream and follow the path ahead through scrub.*

Within a fenced area on your left is a segment of the old Roman road which once ran from Lewes to London. It was excavated in 1939 to expose the iron cinder surface layer, a by-product of the Wealden iron-smelting industry which was already established when the road was constructed in the 2nd Century AD.

A clear path continues up to the A264. Turn left along the grass verge for the short distance back to the start.

Bolebrook Castle.

Walk 5

CAMP HILL

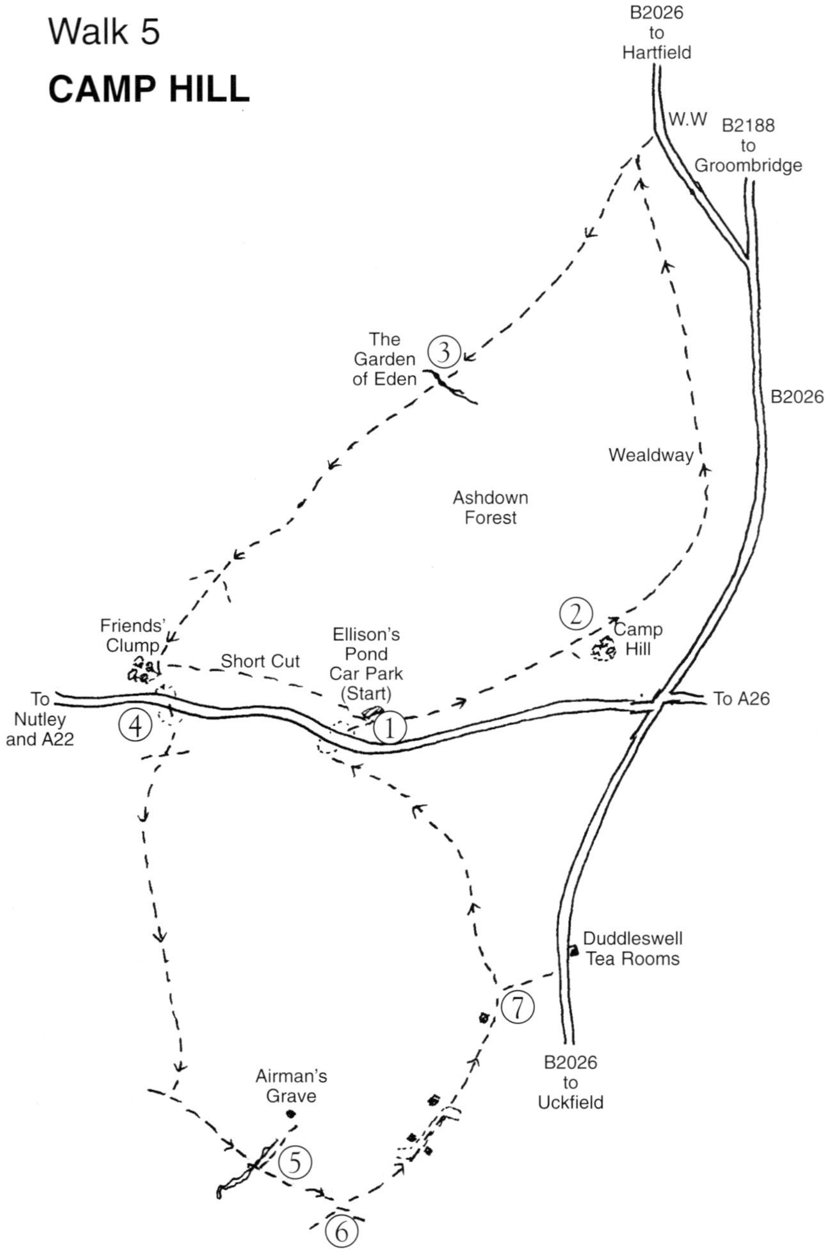

Walk 5

CAMP HILL

Distance:	5 miles
Route:	Ellison's Pond Car Park - Camp Hill - Wealdway - Garden of Eden - Friends' Clump - Airman's Grave - Ellison's Pond Car Park.
Map:	OS Explorer 135: Ashdown Forest
Start/ Parking:	Ellison's Pond car park on the south side of the Camp Hill-to-Nutley road at GR 462287.
Public Transport:	None convenient
Conditions:	Entirely on well-defined forest rides and tracks. Two short and sharp climbs.
Refreshments:	Duddleswell Tea Rooms, a short distance off the route beyond point 7.

Ashdown Forest was once a Royal Hunting Forest covering 14,000 acres. The present reduced area of 6,400 acres is still the largest area of lowland heath in southeast England. Now owned by East Sussex County Council and managed by a Board of Conservators, the whole area is open for public access on foot, mostly unrestricted, though in recent years, cattle and sheep grazing, necessary to resist scrub invasion and allow the re-establishment of some fine expanses of heather has, sadly, led to the erection of many new fences.

Our walk, however, keeps to the open forest following, for the most part, clear, unencumbered forest tracks and rides. Starting and finishing across high open heath on the top of the Forest and offering a series of superb views southwards to the distant South Downs, it is an exceptional walk which doesn't involve a single fence or stile crossing.

THE WALK

To orientate yourself for the start of the walk, stand in the car park entrance with your back to the road **(1)**. *Now head half right past a seat on your right to join a forest track with Ellison's Pond on your left. Follow this wide track as it climbs gently, running roughly parallel to the road, away to your right. As you climb your first objective comes into view ahead, the prominent tree clump on Camp Hill.*

This is one of a number of clumps of conifers, mainly Scots Pine, planted as ornamental features at various points on the top of the forest, most of them originating in the 18th century. In front of the Camp Hill clump is a plaque commemorating the opening of the Wealdway long-distance path in 1981, a section of which we shall be following for the next mile or so.

At the clump **(2)** *go ahead, leaving the trees to your right. The track continues round the head of a valley, rising gently to contour along the gorse and heather-covered slope. After about a mile, just short of a gate, turn sharply back to the left along another wide track. The second tree clump passed on the walk, and the path leading*

Cattle grazing beside Ellison's Pond.

Camp Hill Clump.

up to it, soon come into view, directly ahead against a backdrop of the distant South Downs. Follow the main ride steadily down into a valley to a stream crossing **(3)**.

The brown colour of the water reminds us that the Forest was once a centre for the extraction of iron ore and the iron-smelting industry built upon it during the 16th and 17th centuries. A few yards to the right of the main path from this point you can seek out a tiny waterfall at a spot picturesquely if somewhat hyperbolically known as the Garden of Eden.

Continue with the main ride over a low rise and down into another dip and another stream crossing. A few yards beyond the stream, where you have a choice of three tracks, yours is the one in the middle. The clump of trees, your immediate objective, is temporarily out of sight but comes into view again after the first sharp climb. Meanwhile a small solitary birch tree on the nearer skyline provides an intermediate direction marker. At the top, in front of the tree clump, a seat provides a convenient rest point.

This is Friends' Clump, a relatively recent addition to the forest clumps, planted in 1973 by the Friends of Ashdown Forest to celebrate Tree Planting Year.

Pass to the left of the clump and through a car park to join the Camp Hill-to-Nutley road **(4)**. *Cross the road and continue through another car park, labelled Stonehill.*

Go over a sleeper bridge to the left of another seat and, shortly, where the path divides, fork right. After a few more yards, go straight over a crossing ride and forward along a similar ride, which starts between two blocks of young, mainly oak, trees. The path soon opens out with a virtually uninterrupted distant downland panorama ahead. After about two thirds of a mile, turn left along a wide crossing track which drops down to cross a stream **(5).**

A path to the left from this point offers a detour to visit the Airman's Grave, a small stone enclosure containing a memorial to the crew of a Wellington bomber which crashed near here in July 1941. Return the same way to point 5.

Once over the stream, carry on uphill, ignoring an immediate right fork and passing through an area of birch and oak woodland. Now some care is needed as there are so many tracks and paths to choose from. A few yards after the track levels out **(6),** *turn left along a narrow crossing path and, after a few yards, go straight over a crossing track laid with perforated concrete strips. Shortly, pass to the right of an isolated house and soon join and go ahead along a metalled drive which passes between two more houses. Where the drive curves to the right, fork left (in effect, straight on), soon joining another drive which passes to the right of yet another house. The drive now ends but a narrow grassy path continues ahead. Where the path divides, fork left. Join a drive briefly which passes one more house and continues as a narrow path. Shortly join and bear left along a wide forest track* **(7).**

View towards Friends' Clump from path between points 2 and 3.

If in need of refreshment a narrow path on the right after 100 yards, winds through gorse to reach the B2026 road within sight of the Duddleswell Tea Rooms. Return the same way.

Resume the walk along the main forest track, ignoring all side and crossing paths and it will bring you to a car park. Cross the road to the Ellison's Pond parking area opposite, back at your starting point.

Airman's grave, point 5.

Walk 6

WYCH CROSS AND STUMBLEWOOD COMMON

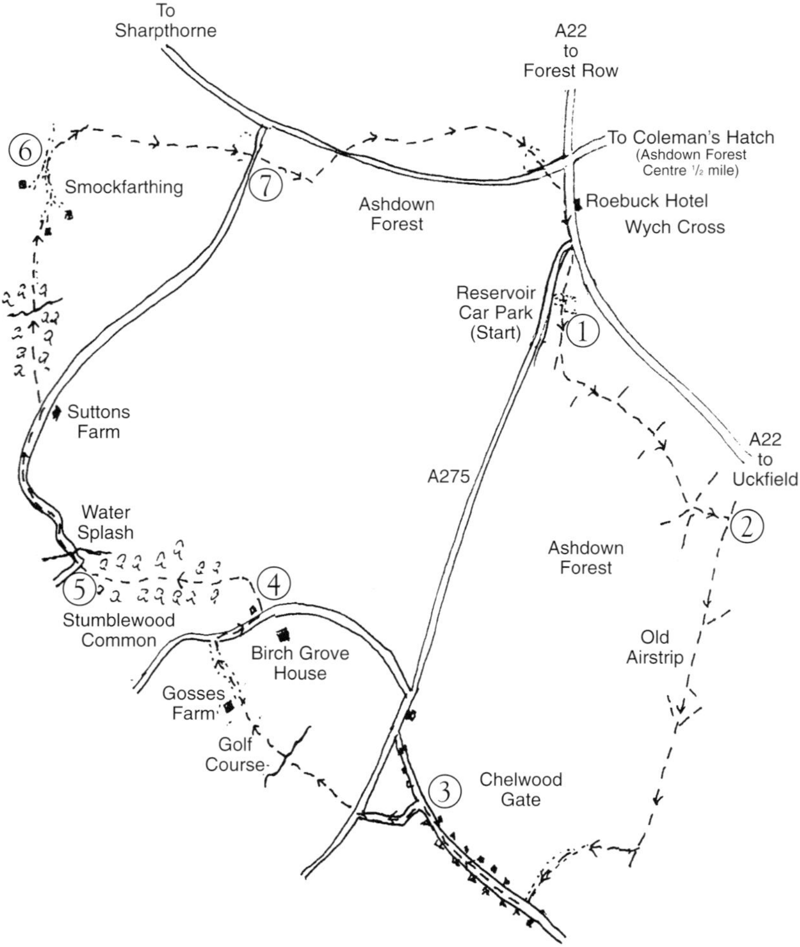

Walk 6

WYCH CROSS AND STUMBLEWOOD COMMON

Distance:	$5^1/_2$ miles
Route:	Wych Cross Reservoir - Old Airstrip - Chelwood Gate - Stumblewood Common - Suttons Farm - Smockfarthing - Wych Cross.
Map:	OS Explorer 135: Ashdown Forest
Start/Parking:	From Wych Cross on the A22 road about two miles south of Forest Row. Park in the parking area beside the short access drive to a covered reservoir to the east of the A275 road about 200 yards south of the A22/A275 junction (GR 419315).
Public Transport:	Bus from Haywards Heath or East Grinstead to Wych Cross, hourly on weekdays, two-hourly on Sundays.
Conditions:	Mostly along sandy forest tracks and established woodland paths. Gentle hills only.
Refreshments:	Red Lion pub at Chelwood Gate, a short distance off the route.

For our second circuit on Ashdown Forest we travel to the western edge of the area for a walk starting and finishing at Wych Cross. After a mile across the open forest the walk leaves the public access area to seek out and explore some fragments of woodland which were once part of the ancient hunting forest but are now detached. The original medieval 'pale' or boundary can still be traced as it passes across Stumblewood Common, a delightful area of ancient woodland which offers one of the highlights of this varied walk.

The route across the open forest presents some navigational challenge, as there are so many alternative paths to lead you astray. If time allows, a preliminary visit to the Ashdown Visitor Centre, about half a mile east of Wych Cross on the Coleman's Hatch road, could prove worthwhile. A map of the Forest, available from the centre, shows all the main paths and rides, including the used route between the start of the walk and Chelwood Gate and beyond point 6. The centre is open from April - September from 2.00pm - 5.00pm (weekdays) and every weekend throughout the year from 11.00am - 5.00pm.

THE WALK

To orientate yourself for the start of the walk, stand with your back to the road, facing the wire mesh entrance gate to the reservoir **(1).** *Turn right along a wide track with the reservoir fence on your left at first. After 50 yards, fork left along a crossing path which heads out across the forest. After a few more yards, where the path divides again, go ahead, ignoring the left fork. Your track soon heads generally south across a fairly open area of gorse and bracken. Stick to the main path, ignoring all side turnings.*

As you proceed, a wide view opens out southwards to a broad sweep of the distant South Downs.

At a point where five tracks converge, go straight ahead and, after another 150 yards or so, turn right along a wide straight forest ride **(2).**

This was cleared and surfaced for use as an emergency landing strip during World War II but few clues to its former use remain, apart from the poor plant growth where the top soil was removed.

Distant view of the South Downs from Ashdown Forest.

Old Airstrip beyond point 2.

Follow this ride, level at first, then gradually losing height. On reaching a bench seat on your left, shaded by small group of conifers, follow the main track round to the right, ignoring a signed horse track ahead. Follow the track down to a stream where it leaves the forest area and continue past houses out to a road at Chelwood Gate. Turn right and after a little over a quarter of a mile, go sharp left along Sandy Lane **(3).**

For the Red Lion pub, carry straight on from point 3 out to the A275 and turn right. Return the same way.

Follow Sandy Lane out to the A275, cross the main road and follow the path opposite which starts over a stile beside a gate, set back from the road, and follows a grassy path down through trees. It takes a straight line as it crosses a golfer's track twice on a bend, marked with white fingerposts, continues down to cross a stream culvert and climbs again. Where the path comes out into the open, go straight ahead across a fairway.

From this open area, you get a glimpse to your right of Birch Grove House, once the home of the former prime minister, Harold Macmillan. To your left a glorious vista opens out southwards across the wooded Weald to the distant South Downs.

Continue along a gravel track past Gosses Farm and on through the golf course to join a road. Turn right. After about 300 yards, just past the gateway to West Watch House on your left **(4),** *turn left along a signed path. At a three-arm fingerpost,*

The pathway through Stumblewood Common.

where you have a choice of two paths, either will do as they both end up at the same place. The left fork provides a gentler gradient. Follow it straight over a crossing path and, where it divides, keep right. The path winds down across the delectable area of Stumblewood Common, a mix of mature trees, mainly oak and silver birch, with an undergrowth of bracken. At the bottom of the hill you will come out to a lane on a bend **(5).**

Turn right across a bridge beside a water splash and follow this quiet lane as it climbs out of the valley for a quarter of a mile. When opposite a gateway entrance, on your right, to Suttons Farm and Tudbridge Gate, turn left along a signed path, overgrown for the first few yards but then much clearer as it drops down through woodland. At the bottom of the hill the path crosses a stream and climbs within the right edge of woodland with a paddock to your right.

Shortly join and go ahead along the concrete drive from stables and, at a junction with another drive coming in from the right, go ahead as it veers right and left. Where another drive joins, this time from the left, continue ahead. After another 100 yards, on reaching a low wooden post to the left of the drive **(6),** *fork right along a grassy path, back on to the open forest.*

After 20 yards, at a path junction, bear left, gently uphill, still on a wide grassy path. After a little over 100 yards, fork right along a level path which contours along the hillside, soon with an intermittent view to the south. Go straight over an oblique crossing path without gaining or losing height. Join a wide track coming in from the right and shortly go ahead, ignoring a track which peels away to the left. Continue along a clear track to reach a car park and picnic area **(7).**

Leave the car park through the right hand exit, cross the road and follow the signed horse track almost opposite. After a little over 200 yards, turn left along a clear path out to the Sharpthorne-to-Wych Cross road. Follow the path opposite which soon bears right across more open forest always within earshot of the traffic on the road away to your right but well insulated from it.

Go straight across a metalled drive and continue along the path opposite which eventually brings you out to the road through a road material storage yard and within yards of Wych Cross. A narrow path, opposite, cuts across the corner to join the A22 south of the crossroads. Bear right beside the main road, passing the Roebuck Hotel on the left. Cross the A275 at its junction with the A22 and follow the path, opposite, which runs parallel and to the left of the A275 back to the start.

Stumblewood Common.

Walk 7

BOARSHEAD, NORTH OF CROWBOROUGH

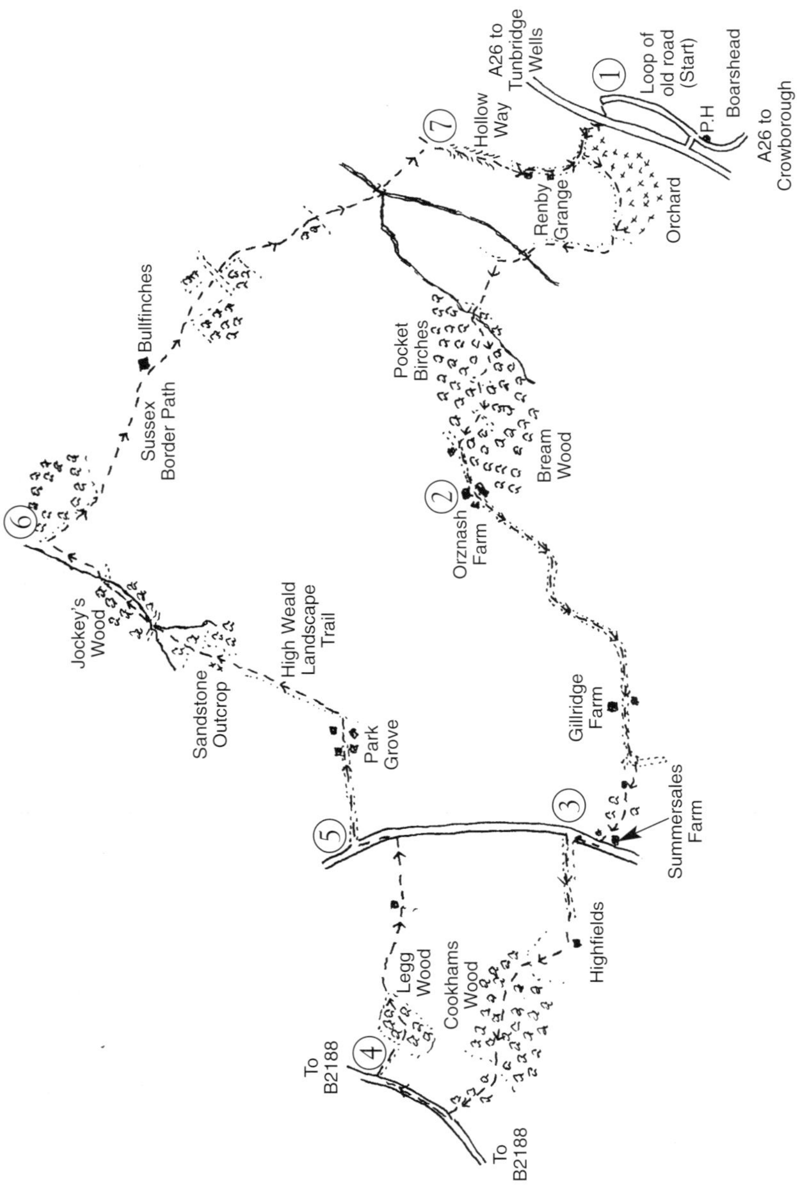

Walk 7

BOARSHEAD, NORTH OF CROWBOROUGH

Distance:	$6^{1}/_{2}$ miles
Route:	Boarshead - Orznash Farm - Summersales Farm - Jockey's Wood - Rock's Farm - Bullfinches - Sussex Border Path - Boarshead.
Map:	OS Explorer 135 - Ashdown Forest.
Start/Parking:	From Boarshead on the A26 Uckfield-to-Tunbridge Wells road about two miles north of Crowborough. Park along a redundant loop of the old A26. The access is signed to Boarshead and the best roadside parking is towards the northern end of this cul-de-sac at GR 536329.
Public Transport:	Bus to Boarshead from Tunbridge Wells or Crowborough.
Conditions:	A moderately strenuous walk with several ups and downs; mostly on good paths.
Refreshments:	Boarshead pub near the start; none on the route.

To the north of Crowborough on the high watershed between the River Rother to the south and east and the River Medway to the north, a series of modest streams drain northwards along wide valleys to join the Medway near Groombridge. Starting high on a ridge, this walk cuts across the grain of the land to follow an undulating route across two of these valleys, before looping northwards along a ridge using part of the High Weald Landscape Trail. It then links with another long distance route, the Sussex Border Path as it turns back across the same valleys further to the north and climbs within a lovely old hollow way back up to Boarshead.

This is a well wooded countryside, offering particular delight in the spring when the predominantly deciduous woods are carpeted with bluebells. The well-drained loam beneath your feet, a mixture of sand and clay in varying proportions, ensures reasonably dry conditions, making this a fine walk for all seasons, right in the geographical centre of the High Weald Area of Outstanding Natural Beauty.

THE WALK

Start the walk between low posts at the northern end of the No Through Road **(1)**. *Cross the new A26 using the ramps provided. At the top of the far ramp turn left along a tree-lined access drive. After a little over 100 yards, fork left along the gravel drive to a house called Lakes Field. Where the drive veers right at the house entrance, go ahead on a rough track.*

Where the track ends at the edge of an orchard, bear right, walking downhill along the right edge. From a stile in the orchard corner a path drops down across undulating pasture. At the bottom of the hill, cross a stream, climb a low bank and bear right along the top of it. Shortly, at a footpath fingerpost, turn left across the middle of a field, descending to enter woodland. Cross a stream and, after a few yards, at a path junction, bear left.

This extensive area of mainly coppiced woodland, marked on the map as Bream Wood and Pocket Birches, is a delectable spot, particularly in the spring at bluebell time.

Orchard near the start.

The path between points 2 and 3.

Climb steadily through the wood, going straight over two crossing tracks. At the top of the hill, at a T-junction, turn left along a hard track past a row of cottages and a converted oast at Orznash Farm **(2)** *and on with good, if intermittent, views back across the valley you have just crossed. Continue past Gillridge Farm and, at the point where a private drive to Stonecroft Farm forks right, go ahead over a stile and across pasture, passing to the left of a group of outbuildings. An enclosed path continues to the right of an equestrian area and on through a wood. At a T-junction, turn right and follow a trodden path, straightforward apart from an awkward barrier in the form of two sets of iron rails on either side of a crossing track between two fields. Continue out past the buildings at Summersales Farm to join a road and turn right.*

After about 100 yards **(3),** *where you have a choice of two parallel drives to the left, yours is the one on the right, the drive to a house called Highfields. About 100 yards short of the house, a narrow fenced path starts, parallel and to the right of the drive. Shortly, go right over a stile and squarely out across a field to enter woodland. Where the path divides, keep right, following a fence on your left. It takes you through more bluebell woods and out to a lane where you should turn right.*

After 300 yards **(4),** *turn right over a stile, now on part of the well waymarked High Weald Landscape Trail. Follow it beside a field, through Legg Wood and on along a left field edge. Carry on past a house in a dip and up across two fields with a stile between them to join a road. Turn left.*

The path through Bream Wood.

After about 200 yards **(5)**, *turn right along the rhododendron-lined drive to Park Grove and other properties. Ignoring a left fork, go ahead along a drive between houses. Beyond a brick gateway go through a field gate and on beside park railings.*

Once through a smart new metal swing gate, turn left along the left field edge to a squeeze stile and on along the ridge, following an intermittent line of trees, mainly silver birch, soon passing to the right of a sandstone outcrop.

This is a modest but quite striking version of the many similar weathered outcrops which are characteristic of this area. Further north at Harrison's Rocks, near Groombridge, they are big enough to be worthy of the attention of rock climbers.

Continue with the High Weald Trail, down through a wood, across a cleared area and on into another wood. Shortly bear right to cross a drive and continue through the wood, down to a stream crossing and on with the stream on your left. In the field corner **(6)** *the High Weald Trail goes off to the left, back over the stream, but you should turn sharply right, soon climbing beside a holly-clad sandstone bank on your left, now on part of the Sussex Border Path*

In the top field corner, go over a stile and head out across a field, passing under power lines, to find the next stile, out of view at first. Maintain direction, following another set of minor power lines across two fields and along the left edge of a third. Pass to the right of a large house at Bullfinches, go over a stile and continue in the same direction downhill to another stile. Continue down, passing to the left of one block of woodland and to the right of another. Cross a track and climb with a third block of woodland on your right.

At the wood corner, veer half right across a field to join and follow the left edge of a small copse. From the corner of the copse go ahead across a field, pass to the right of a tree clump, go through a hedge gap and veer slightly right down across the field beyond. In the bottom right field corner, go over a stile and bear right along a hedged track which soon climbs steeply up out of the valley. At a T-junction **(7)** *turn right and follow another track which soon enters a fine old hollow way.*

It finally emerges into the open at an excellent viewpoint from which to look back across the valley to Bullfinches and the mass of Bream Wood, traversed on the outward leg of the walk.

Go forward for a few yards then left over a stile to join a drive. Turn right and follow the drive past Renby Grange and on out to the A26, rejoining your outgoing route for the last few yards. Walk back across the main road to the start.

Sandstone Outcrop beyond point 5.

Walk 8

FORDCOMBE, SPELDHURST AND THE MEDWAY VALLEY

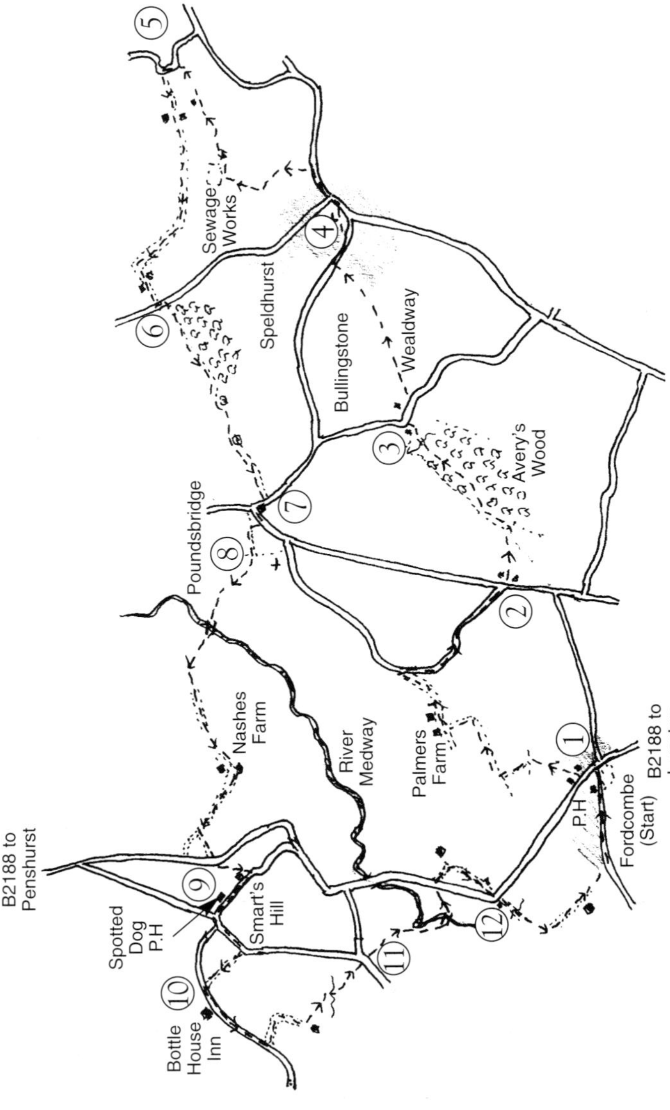

Walk 8

FORDCOMBE, SPELDHURST AND THE MEDWAY VALLEY

Distance:	8½ miles
Route:	Fordcombe - Palmers Farm - Wealdway - Speldhurst - Poundsbridge - Nashes Farm - Smart's Hill - Bottle House Inn - Fordcombe.
Map:	OS Explorer 147: Sevenoaks and Tonbridge.
Start/Parking:	From Fordcombe on the B2188 road which heads north from the A264 Tunbridge Wells-to-East Grinstead road about 3 miles west of Tunbridge Wells. The B2188 is wide enough to allow roadside parking in the vicinity of the village green, avoiding the bus stops and with due care not to impede access of local residents. (GR 527403)
Public Transport:	Approximately two-hourly weekday bus service to Fordcombe from Tunbridge Wells.
Conditions:	Mostly easy going along good tracks and paths. Some mud likely during the winter months. Gently undulating terrain plus one sharp climb to Smart's Hill.
Refreshments:	Pubs at Fordcombe and Speldhurst and two more at Smart's Hill.

Less than half a mile into the walk, a superb panoramic view opens out across the Medway valley towards Penshurst (Walk 3). It then picks a route through commuter country to the north and west of Tunbridge Wells, though retaining a rural character as it seeks out a series of long established paths, often lined by trees and high banks, which wind between the landscaped gardens and desirable residences around Speldhurst. The walk then heads westwards along the slopes of another wide and beautiful valley formed by a feeder stream leading to a crossing of the Medway. The return route takes a wide loop to the west, climbing steeply up to Smart's Hill where there is a choice of two pubs within half a mile, conveniently placed about two-thirds of the way round the circuit.

THE WALK

From the offset crossroads next to Fordcombe village green **(1),** *start the walk westwards along the B2188, signposted to Penshurst, Leigh and Tonbridge. After a few yards, just past a bus shelter on the left, turn right along a signposted footpath which starts as a wide grass strip between fence and wall. Where the path ends, go straight ahead across a large field, where a path should be trodden out through any growing crop, to a stile and downhill along a left field edge. In the field corner go ahead over a stile and immediately turn right along a right field edge.*

From here a wide vista opens out northwards across the Medway valley with the 14th Century manor house, Penshurst Place, in view directly ahead.

Walk round two sides of this field, dropping down to find a gap in the hedge in the bottom right hand corner. Bear half right across a small field to a waypost and down steps to join a track in front of a cottage. Turn right to follow this track between the

Footbridge over the stream in Avery's Wood.

Speldhurst Churchyard.

buildings of Palmers Farm and on to join a lane where you should turn sharply back to the right, uphill. After a steady climb for the best part of half a mile, at a road junction **(2),** *go over a stile ahead.*

From here to Speldhurst you will be following one of the most attractive sections of the Wealdway, a long distance route linking the Thames Estuary at Gravesend with the English Channel at Eastbourne.

Follow this trodden, well stiled and well waymarked path through trees, across two fields and on through Avery's Wood where it descends to cross a stream in a delectable wooded dell before climbing steeply. At a path junction at the top of this steep slope, go left out to a lane at Bullingstone **(3).** *Turn right.*

For the next half a mile the Wealdway shares a route with the confusingly similarly named High Weald Walk, a 28-mile circular route round Tunbridge Wells.

After 100 yards along the lane, go left along a fenced path which you can follow, unmistakeably, for half a mile out to join a road at Speldhurst. Turn right and, very shortly, a few yards short of the George and Dragon pub, go left through the lych gate into Speldhurst churchyard.

The solid sandstone church dates entirely from 1870 and is notable for stained glass by William Morris and Edward Burne-Jones.

Poundsbridge Church, point 8.

Pass to the right of the church **(4)** *and leave the churchyard down a steep flight of steps. Turn left and, after a few yards, keep right with the main road, signposted to Southborough and Tunbridge Wells. After about 200 yards, turn left along a signed footpath which starts to the right of a drive to a house called Parkview. Follow an enclosed path along the side of a valley to join a concrete drive and turn right. At the entrance gate to a sewage treatment works, turn right over a stile and follow a left field edge until you can go left over a footbridge and a wooden causeway across a swampy area. A path continues up through woodland to a T-junction with a roughly metalled access drive where you should turn left.*

After a few yards go right up stone steps to follow another enclosed path to a stile and continue gently up along a left field edge until you can go left over a stile and along another short enclosed path out to a lane (5). Turn left and, after about 100 yards, go left again over a stile and forward along the left edge of two fields.

From this path you can enjoy a fine open view northwards towards Bidborough on the ridge opposite.

In the field corner go forward, cross stone steps to the right of a gate and continue along a farm track.

Another view soon opens out, this time to the left, back across the valley to the square tower of Speldhurst church on the skyline.

Follow this drive downhill, across a stream and on along the valley with the stream on your right. Continue with the drive as it bears round to the left, past two rows of cottages and out to a road **(6).** *Turn left and, after a few yards, go right along a clear path, fenced at first then along a left field edge with woodland to your left. Go over a plank bridge a few yards to the right of the field corner and continue along the left edge of another field. Skirt to the right of a pond and go ahead, passing between two double power poles to find another stile. Pass to the right of another pond and continue along a left field edge out to a lane* **(7).**

Turn right and, after a few yards at a road junction, go left, passing a fine old timber-framed house with an inscribed date on its wall, 1593. After less than 100 yards go right over a stile, across grass to a second stile and then left beside a hedge to cross a stile beside a gate **(8).**

A short detour up the hill to the left from this point allows a visit to the simple late Victorian chapel at Poundsbridge, occupying a grand situation, overlooking the Medway valley.

From point 8 go half right across a low-lying meadow to another gate and on with a drainage ditch on your right. Cross the Medway, climb beside a fence and continue along a track, hedged at first then across a field to pass between the buildings at Nashes Farm. Follow the main drive from the farm until, just short of a red brick cottage on

View towards Penshurst Place from Smart's Hill.

the left, you can turn left along a right field edge to join the B2188 (Care- fast traffic and blind bend!). Turn left and, after a few yards **(9)** *go right up steps. A well trodden path winds up through an area of rough pasture and scrub to join another road.*

From the top of this steep slope pause for breath and to look back across the Medway and along the valley towards Speldhurst, a fine vista.

Turn right along the road, soon passing the Spotted Dog pub.

This popular 15th Century pub, with its extensive terraced garden, occupies an enviable position overlooking the Medway valley and offers a further excuse for a rest after the stiff climb up from the river.

At a road junction, go ahead, signposted to Chiddingstone and Cowden and, after a few more yards, fork left along Nunnery Lane. After 200 yards or so, turn right along a fenced footpath which takes you through to another road where you should turn left past another bustling hostelry, the Bottle House Inn **(10).** *After another 300 yards, turn left along a metalled drive, signposted as a footpath. Follow this drive as it bends round to the right and drops downhill.*

Hairpin loop in the River Medway between points 11 and 12.

After about 200 yards, fork left up a ramped access to a gate and go ahead, dropping down across a field to go through a makeshift hurdle gate and contour along the lower hillside with a stream in a wooded gully to your right. Shortly bear right, dropping steeply to cross a footbridge over the stream. Now turn left along the valley beside a left hand fence out to a road **(11).**

Your next path starts over the stile opposite. Follow an intermittent line of mature oak trees across a field and on in the same direction down to a footbridge. Now go half right across a meadow to join the River Medway at a point where it makes a hairpin loop. Follow the riverbank until you can go left across it and left again across a field to join the B2188. Follow the drive to Fordcombe Manor, opposite. At a T-junction turn right along another drive, past several houses and on to rejoin the B2188 **(12).**

Turn left and after 20 yards turn right along an enclosed path which you can follow across a stream and up again. Where the fenced path ends at a stile, go ahead along the right edge of a grassy area, once an orchard, now reduced to a scanty group of ancient fruit trees. Join and go ahead along the drive from Chafford Farm out to a lane. Turn left for about a quarter of a mile back to Fordcombe.

Walk 9

LAMBERHURST, GOUDHURST AND THE TEIZE VALLEY

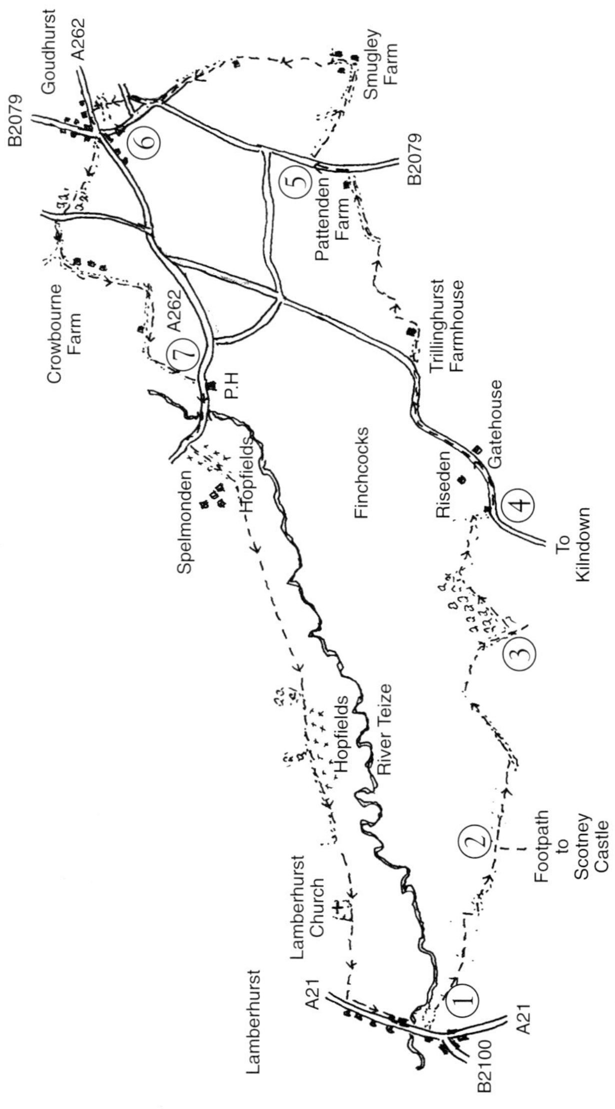

Walk 9

LAMBERHURST, GOUDHURST AND THE TEIZE VALLEY

Distance:	8 miles
Route:	Lamberhurst - Riseden - Pattenden Farm - Goudhurst - Crowbourne Farm - Spelmonden - Lamberhurst.
Map:	OS Explorer 136: The Weald
Start/Parking:	From Lamberhurst on the A21 London-to-Hastings road. Park in the free car park, signposted eastwards from the High Street almost opposite the junction of the A21 and the B2100 at GR 677362.
Public Transport:	Occasional weekday bus service from Tunbridge Wells to Lamberhurst.
Conditions:	Straightforward walking, mostly along field paths or good tracks. Some risk of flooding during the winter months at the start and finish of the walk. Gentle hills only.
Refreshments:	Pubs at Lamberhurst. Pubs and tea room at Goudhurst. Pub at point 7.

This walk offers a varied perspective of the wide and beautiful valley of the Teize, a river which rises deep in the High Weald to the east of Tunbridge Wells before flowing eastwards and northwards to join the Medway. The outgoing route of our walk traverses the southern slopes of this valley, passing through the Scotney Estate before climbing gently to Goudhurst, a beautifully situated hilltop village, where the High Street is lined by a rich variety of old houses, many weatherboarded and tile hung, and the solid sandstone church occupies a prime site on the top of the hill. Leaving the village, you can enjoy a spectacular view along the whole length of the Teize valley. The return route drops down to take a direct low level route along the valley back to

Lamberhurst, another pleasant village which will be even more attractive when a long-awaited bypass is finally built.

THE WALK

From the far end of the car park ***(1),*** *go straight ahead across a recreation area and sports ground, passing between two football pitches to go through a gap in the hedge in the far right corner behind the goal posts of the right hand pitch. Go forward across a golf fairway to a stile and on beside a right hand hedge. Very shortly, where this hedge ends, go ahead across the golf playing area, passing to the right of a tee to find a gap in a row of young planted trees. Go forward across a small field, bear right to cross a concrete drive and go ahead with a hedge on your left. After 60 yards go left through a wide gap and bear half right uphill along a right field edge with a wood on your right.*

In the top field corner, go right over a stile, forward along a left field edge for 40 yards, then left over a second stile and ahead beside a fence to reach a three-arm fingerpost ***(2).***

Scotney Castle can be reached along the footpath to the right, adding about a mile to the walk and returning the same way. The gardens and the picturesque ruins of the old castle, a National Trust property, are open during the summer months except on Mondays and Tuesdays. For detailed opening times telephone 01892 891081.

Lamberhurst Church from across the valley near point 2.

Goudhurst Village street.

To continue the walk go straight ahead across pasture from point 2, signposted to Kilndown. Go over a stile beside a gate and forward along a left field edge.

From this path you get a fine view to the right across the well wooded Scotney Estate. The Castle ruins are hidden by trees, but you get a glimpse of the Victorian house nearby which houses the local headquarters of the National Trust.

In the field corner join a drive and turn left, soon ignoring the signed path to Kilndown which goes off to the right.

From this drive the hilltop village of Goudhurst, our next objective, comes into view ahead.

After a little over 300 yards, go right over a stile and follow the direction of a waymark down across a field to a gate from which a wide sandy track continues. After another 200 yards, at a waypost **(3),** *turn left along a left field edge with a wood on your left, following a permissive National Trust path. Towards the end of the field, ignore a stile into the wood. After a few yards, in the field corner, go right up a bank and, after 20 yards, left over a stile. After a few more paces, go right over a second stile and head out across a paddock, diverging at about 30 degrees from the fence on your left. Rejoin the left field edge for a few yards as it juts out towards you from the left and then continue across grass without change of direction. In the far right field corner, go over a stile, down a flight of concrete steps and turn right along an enclosed path which takes you out to a lane* **(4).**

Goudhurst Church.

Double back sharply along the lane and, after a little over half a mile, turn right along a concrete drive, marked with a green plaque as part of a local millennium walk which we shall be following as far as point 7, similarly waymarked at various points. The path skirts to the right of a converted twin oast and then bears left along a field edge with Goudhurst now prominently in view directly ahead.

In the field corner follow the fence round to the right, staying within the same field and ignoring a path off to the left over a stile into an orchard. In the next field corner go through a white gate and turn left round two sides of a field. In the field corner bear left for a few yards to go through a gateway and across a culvert. Now head squarely across a field to an elaborate step stile in a bank. Veer half left across grass to join a track and turn left through another white gate, Now follow the drive for 300 yards, out past the buildings at Pattenden Farm to join the B2079 road and turn left.

After less than 200 yards **(5)** *turn right along a roughly metalled drive, signposted as a public footpath. Beyond a stile, where the drive peters out, go forward along a left field edge to another stile and follow minor power lines across the next field. Join and go ahead along a tarmac drive (not the parallel gravel track to the right). Immediately in front of The South Oast, an elaborate and elegant conversion, turn left with the drive. Continue with the drive until you can fork left at a waypost along a wide grassy*

The view from Goudhurst Churchyard.

path. Follow waymarks as your path doglegs left between concrete gate posts, then right along a track laid with concrete sleepers at first, then with a pleasant grass surface.

Reaching a metalled drive on a corner by a house, go left for five yards, then right over a stile and gently uphill along a right field edge. Walk across a sandy equestrian exercise area where you must squeeze through narrow gaps in the wooden boundary fence. Go over a stile and go left uphill along a drive.

Join and go right along Maypole Lane. At a road junction, double back to the left along Tiddymotts Lane and after a few yards go right up steps and along a fenced path which takes you through to another lane. Go up more steps, almost opposite and walk out through Goudhurst churchyard into the village **(6).**

Here is a place to linger and enjoy, not only to sample the pubs or tea rooms but to appreciate the 14th Century church, a row of Weaver's Cottages facing the churchyard and Church House, nearby, once the home of a master weaver, both reminders of the cloth-weaving industry which once flourished locally.

From the main church entrance walk ahead down the village High Street. At a cross roads next to the Vine Hotel, go ahead along a gravel drive which starts immediately to the right of the village war memorial. It narrows to a path through scrub to reach a stile.

At this point a magnificent view opens out ahead across the valley of the River Teize as it feeds northwards into the Medway to the west of Tonbridge, a panorama of the 'Garden of England' once a patchwork of orchards, though the industry is now in steady decline, reduced by over a third in the last 40 years.

Two trodden paths drop down the slope ahead, keep to the one on the left, along the left edge of rough pasture and scrub to a stile and on through a wood to join a lane. Follow the drive opposite to Hammonds and Crowbourne and, where it divides, fork left, signed to Crowbourne Farm. Follow the drive as it skirts to the right of a large house until you can go right through a bridle gate. A path, well waymarked, skirts to the right of several gardens and then heads out across a field. Go left through a gate and, after five yards right along another clear grassy path.

At a T-junction with a metalled access drive, turn right and, immediately fork left over a half-hidden stile beside a gate. Follow a right field edge, walking round two sides of the field. Just short of the second field corner go right over a stile and along an enclosed path out to the A262 road **(7).** *Turn right past the Green Cross Inn. After about 300 tiresome yards beside this busy road, turn left over a stile beside a gate and go ahead along a concrete track.*

You are now passing between hop fields, an increasingly rare sight nowadays. Hop fields have flourished in Kent for 400 years but are now, like the orchards,

View along Teize valley from path beyond Goudhurst.

in rapid decline, the main evidence of this once-flourishing industry being the white-cowled oasts, now mostly converted into residences.

Where the concrete drive bears right towards the farm complex at Spelmonden, go straight ahead across grass to a gate and on in the same direction across the next field to another gate. Follow the right edge of the next field to a stile and head out across the field beyond, aiming for the left end of a block of woodland. Maintain your direction to go through a gate about 30 yards to the right of the next field corner and ahead, walking beside a right hand fence.

The imposing Georgian House in view across the fields to your left is Finchcocks, built in 1725. It now houses a historic collection of keyboard instruments. The house is accessible along a drive from point 7 on this walk and is open to the public by appointment and on certain days during the summer. For more information telephone 01580 211702.

In the field corner, where you have a choice of two gates ahead, go through the one to the left and on with a high shelter belt hedge on your right and the spire of Lamberhurst church in view ahead. In the field corner go through a gap and along the right hand edge of another hop field where, half way along, the track acquires a concrete surface.

Where this track bends away to the right, go ahead across a footbridge and across two more fields to reach the corner of Lamberhurst churchyard. The path skirts to the left of the churchyard at first and then runs just inside its left hand edge. Follow the tarmac path from the church until, just short of the A21, you can turn left along a pleasant tree lined path, well segregated from the busy main road, down the hill and back to the start.

Walk 10

CRANBROOK

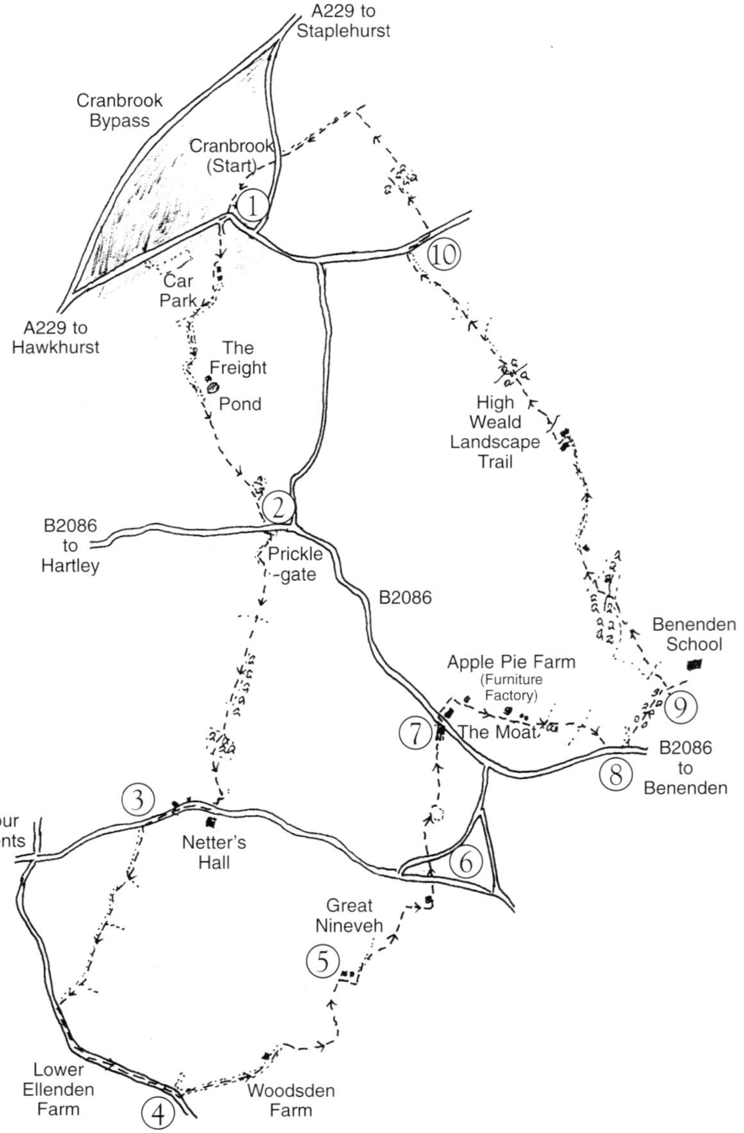

Walk 10
CRANBROOK

Distance:	$8^3/_4$ miles
Route:	Cranbrook - The Freight - Pricklegate - Netter's Hall - Lower Ellenden Farm - Great Nineveh - The Moat - Benenden School - High Weald Landscape Trail - Cranbrook.
Map:	OS Explorer 136: The Weald, plus a very small section of OS Explorer 125: Romney Marsh.
Start/Parking:	From Cranbrook, bypassed by, and signposted from, the A227 Hawkhurst-to-Staplehurst road. Park in the long-stay car park at GR 776359.
Public Transport:	Hourly weekday bus service from Maidstone, Hawkhurst, Battle and Hastings.
Conditions:	Much of the walk is along field paths, some little used.
Refreshments:	Pubs and tea rooms at Cranbrook.

The phrase 'Garden of England' conjures up a landscape of orchards, hop fields and oast houses and would, at one time have been an accurate description of the countryside explored on this walk from Cranbrook. Sadly, the orchards have been reduced to modest fragments, the hop fields are almost gone and the oast houses have been converted to up-market country residences.

The walk is still a beautiful one, through lush meadows and small isolated pockets of woodland, passing a number of farms and substantial country houses but avoiding all settlements, once it is way from the busy little town of Cranbrook.

Some of the paths on the outgoing section of the walk are little used and poorly signed so navigation requires particular care. Fortunately, the return route from Benenden School follows the well maintained and waymarked High Weald Landscape Trail.

Cranbrook Church.

THE WALK

To orientate yourself for the start of the walk, go to the bend in Cranbrook High Street and stand with your back to the steps up into the churchyard **(1).** *Go right along the High Street and shortly, just past the Post Office on your left, turn left along a 'No Through Road', which becomes a tarmac path as it winds down through a landscaped area to a footbridge and up again.*

Just short of the point where the path joins the end of an estate road, turn right along a crossing path and, after 15 yards, go left along a narrower path, soon between high hedges. Join and go forward along Bramley Drive for a few yards only before bearing right along a gravel drive, and then left where the drive acquires a tarmac surface.

Ignoring a right fork (the drive to Mount Ephraim Farm), carry on along the drive as it doglegs right and left and continues between old orchards. Where it divides, keep right (virtually straight on). Drop down gently to cross a dam at the head of an attractive ornamental pond on your left. The drive now becomes a grassy path which climbs across a field. Walk through a belt of trees and ahead along the left edge of a large field. Where the hedge boundary on your left ends abruptly, go ahead without change of direction, aiming for the right corner of woodland where you join and follow a left field edge, leaving the wood on your left. Follow this headland and a short woodland path out to join the B2086 road **(2).**

Go through a narrow gap in the hedge opposite and walk left round two sides of a

Pond at The Freight.

field until you can go left over a stile in the hedge. Now, similarly, walk right round two sides of a field, part orchard, part arable, until you can go right over another stile and forward with a hedge, left. After about 150 yards, sidestep to the left through a hedge gap and right, resuming your previous direction with the hedge now on your right. Where the hedge ends, go ahead across a field to a stile, in sight, and on across the field beyond, continuing along a left field edge with a belt of trees on your left.

From this path which follows a low descending ridge, a fine view opens out ahead, southwards towards Hawkhurst, with its prominent church spire.

The path drops down along a left field edge and on through an area of woodland. After a short overgrown section of path, go right to leave the wood and left along the wood edge. Where the wood ends, continue across a field to join a deeply sunken track over a stile. Turn right along this track out to a lane opposite Netters Hall, a rather grand country house, and turn right to follow the lane across a valley and up again.

At the bottom you will cross a tiny stream, a minor tributary of the Rother, rising to the south of Cranbrook and flowing south-eastwards to join the main river near the Isle of Oxney (Walk 14).

After about 350 yards, as the lane passes beneath major power lines **(3),** *turn left to a gate, walk through a dip and climb along the right edge of two fields. Go straight ahead across a third field and continue along the right edge of three more fields to join a road. Turn left.*

After about half a mile, soon after crossing a stream and passing a flood warning notice **(4),** *fork left along the second of two driveways, the one to Park Farm and Woodsden Farm. Where the drive ends beyond Woodsden Farm house, turn right in front of a green gate. Shortly go through a metal squeeze stile and along a left field edge. Use a second squeeze stile to get through the hedge on your left and resume your previous direction, now with the hedge on your right.*

In the field corner go through another green gate and turn left along a left field edge, passing successively under major and minor power lines. Cross a culverted stream in a wooded dip and head out across a field, aiming for a solitary waypost where you should turn left, walking beneath power lines to a stile and along the right edge of a meadow.

Go through a gate and forward between the outbuildings at Great Nineveh **(5)***. After a few yards, turn right along the right edge of the farm complex with a post and*

View towards Hawkhurst from path beyond point 2.

rail fence to your right. Go through a gate and turn squarely left to follow the left edge of a field until you can go left through a gate and continue along an enclosed path. Beyond a stile, go half right across a large field to find another isolated waypost where you can bear left along an unfenced track across high ground. After 250 yards, follow the direction of waymarks right along a left field edge for 100 yards, then left over a stile and along a left field edge out to a lane **(6).**

Your next path starts almost opposite over a stile beside a gate and heads out across a field to join another lane. Once again, your next path starts opposite, up a wooded bank and on beside a hedge. Skirt to the left of a small cleared area of woodland to find a stile and head slightly left across the field beyond to join and follow a left field edge to a stile and along the left edge of a garden to join the B2086 **(7).** *Turn left and, after a few yards, go right along a drive which runs to the left of a high fence surrounding a large house called The Moat. After less than 100 yards, go right through a gateway and forward, skirting to the right of a large courtyard with The Moat to your right. Your path takes a straight course through a landscaped area and an orchard before skirting to the right of the buildings at Apple Pie Farm, now a furniture factory.*

At a drive, go left for a few yards, then right, resuming your previous direction and skirting to the right of two bungalows, along a left field edge. In the field corner go left through a gap and right along a fenced path, resuming your easterly progress, soon along the left edge of three paddocks. Beyond a double stile, veer slightly right across a meadow to rejoin the B2086 and turn left.

After about 100 yards **(8),** *fork left along the drive to Mounts Farm and, almost immediately, fork right through a swing gate and go ahead along an avenue of lime trees, partly mature, partly replanted. Pass behind a small games pavilion and forward over a stile beside a gate* **(9),** *before turning left to cross a second stile.*

A short walk ahead from point 9 allows an excellent view of Benenden School, an imposing Elizabethan-style mansion, built for Viscount Cranbrook in 1859 and constructed in brick and sandstone. Return the same way.

From the second stile mentioned above, head out across pasture to a third stile and then down, without change of direction, aiming for a corner of woodland jutting out into the field from the left.

For the rest of the walk you will be following part of the High Weald Landscape Trail, well waymarked and showing signs of regular use, making navigation simpler than along some of the more neglected paths on the earlier stages of the walk.

Join and follow the right wood edge. From a stile in the field corner, the path runs within the wood edge before dropping down to a stream and up again. After leaving the wood, go ahead across a meadow to enter an enclosed path which, beyond a pleasant brick and tile-hung cottage, becomes a driveway. After a quarter of a mile, at a T-junction in front of a large poultry house, go left for a few yards, then right past the end of the building.

Pass to the left of a curious isolated brick fireplace and chimney and wind down through a wood to a footbridge. After leaving the trees a well marked path heads squarely out across an arable field to join and follow a left field edge before plunging down through another wooded dip and up steps to a stile.

Continue along a left field edge. Just short of the field corner, sidestep to the left through a gap and turn right beside a right hand hedge. In the next field, diverge very slightly from the fence on your right to find a stile next to a field corner jutting out towards you. Keep to the left of the next two fields, then along the right edge of an orchard to join a road and turn right.

After about 200 yards **(10)** *go left over a stile and squarely across a field. Go through a wide gap in a hedge and along a right field edge. Cross a stream, climb through a glade of willow trees and bear right along a right field edge. After less than 100 yards, turn left along a wide grassy strip between two fields. At a T-junction with an enclosed path, turn left and follow it beside a perimeter fence surrounding parkland to your right. Cross a road and continue beside a recreation ground. Walk out through Cranbrook churchyard to the High Street.*

The church is an imposing structure with a striking clerestory roof above the nave. Cranbrook is a bustling little town well worth exploring if time and energy permit.

Benenden School.

Walk 11

STONEGATE AND THE LIMDEN VALLEY

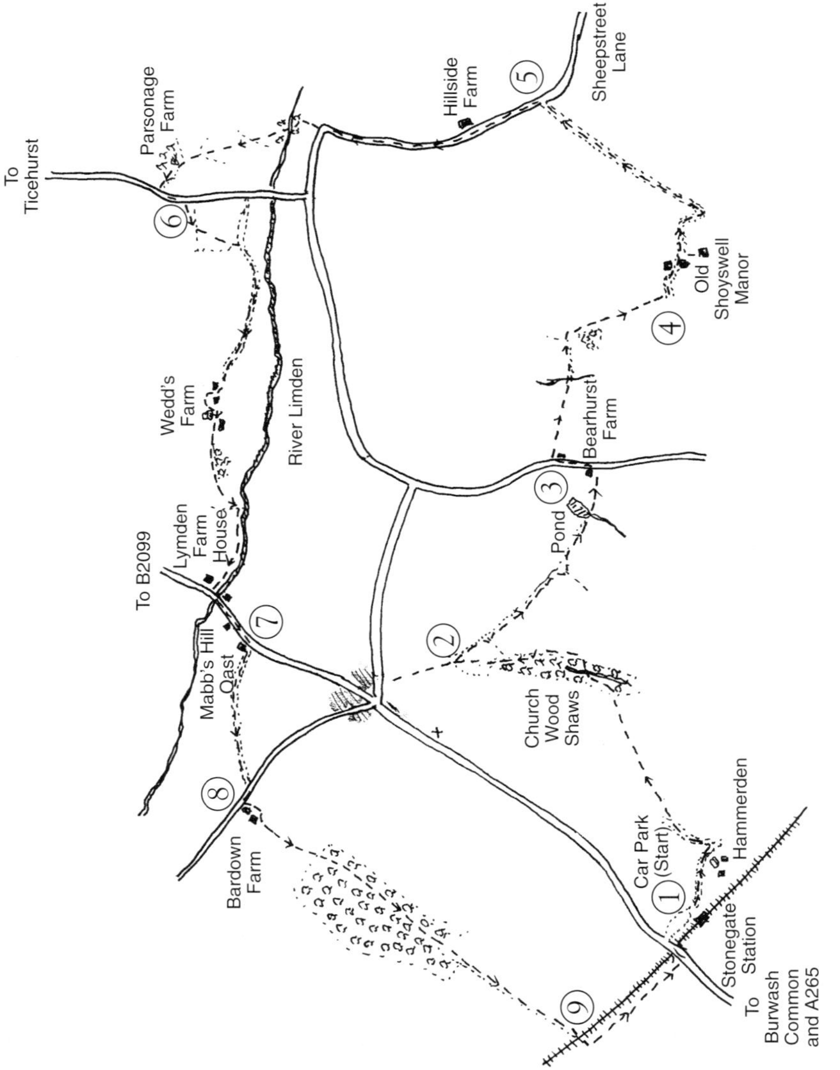

Walk 11

STONEGATE AND THE LIMDEN VALLEY

Distance:	7 miles
Route:	Stonegate Station - Church Wood Shaws - Bearhurst Farm - Old Shoyswell Manor - Hillside Farm - Parsonage Farm - Wedd's Farm - Bardown - Stonegate Station.
Map:	OS Explorer 136: The Weald
Start/Parking:	From Stonegate Station which is signposted northwards from the A265 Heathfield-to-Hurst Green road at Burwash Common. The station car park is free at weekends. Fee payable Monday to Friday when the car park may be full. Privately run 'overflow' car park a few yards to the south. (GR 658272)
Public Transport:	Train service to Stonegate on the Hastings-to-Tunbridge Wells line.
Conditions:	Field and woodland paths plus three-quarters of a mile along a quiet lane. One muddy track.
Refreshments:	None.

The modest River Limden is one of the main tributary streams of the River Rother, flowing westwards through a remote and beautiful valley to the south of Ticehurst before turning south to feed into the main river near Etchingham.

The walk starts from the conveniently placed rural railway station at Stonegate in the Rother valley but quickly climbs to cross the ridge separating the Rother from the Limden before dropping down to explore the Limden valley, passing a number of isolated farmhouses, often incorporating converted oasts.

You will pass a variety of ponds on this walk, some newly excavated as an ornamental feature and still rather raw, though they will surely mellow with time. Others, often hidden by trees, and likely to be dry during the summer months, are old pits, from which iron ore was once excavated, a relic of the industry which flourished in the area during earlier centuries.

THE WALK

Pond at Hammerden

From the far end of the station car park **(1)** *follow a concrete farm drive to Hammerden where it curves right, with a pond on your right. Just past the pond, turn sharply back to the left along a hedged track. When you have a choice of two gates ahead, go through the one on the right and head out diagonally across a large field to go through another gate to the left of a pond surrounded by trees. Continue in the same direction across the next field to a stile from which a path winds on through a wood, descending to cross a stream. Climb to leave the wood and turn left along the left edge of two fields until a stile on the left allows you back into the wood. Bear right on a path parallel to the wood edge. Leave the wood over another stile and go ahead across undulating pasture. Just short of a stile beside a gate* **(2),** *turn sharply back to the right, staying within the same field. In the field corner go through a metal gate and continue beside the next field.*

From this path you get a fine view to your right, southwards across the broad valley of the River Rother to the hilltop village of Burwash, the starting point of Walk 12.

Pond between points 2 and 3.

In the field corner divert a few yards to the right to find a way through the hedge and resume your previous direction along the left edge of two more fields. In the second field corner, another minor 20-yard detour to the right is necessary to find a stile (broken) and a narrow path through a belt of scrub. Keep to the left of the next field, dropping down to cross the outflow from a pond on your left, then follow a drive uphill and out to a road. Turn left.

After about 300 yards **(3),** *just short of a row of cottages on the right (Layhall Cottage), turn right through a gate and go ahead along a left field edge. Where the fence on your left turns away to your left, go ahead across a field to a stile. Veer very slightly right down across the next field, cross a culverted stream and stile and climb beside a right hand hedge. At the top of the hill go over a stile and head squarely out across the next field to a gate which comes into sight as you go over a low summit. Beyond this gate, turn right along a right field edge with a small wood on your right. From the corner of the wood, continue in the same direction down across a large field to join a farm track through a gate* **(4).** *Follow this track between farm buildings and on past the stately gateway to Old Shoyswell Manor.*

This fine old timber-framed manor house occupies a beautiful setting, surrounded by a landscaped garden and, in the grounds, a nicely converted oast house.

Follow the main drive from the manor as it wobbles right and left and continues along the side of the valley, gently climbing for over a quarter of a mile to join a road (Sheepstreet Lane) **(5).** *Turn left and follow this quiet lane for half a mile.*

Approaching Old Shoyswell Manor.

The road carries little traffic and, as you proceed, a view opens out ahead across the Limden valley with Ticehurst church identifiable on high ground to the north.

Where the road begins to drop steeply and hairpins to the left, go ahead over a stile and drop down across pasture to enter woodland over an awkward stepless stile. Once inside the wood, bear left, down between banks. Cross the Limden stream, go through a gate and head out half left across a field to another gate. Continue, without change of direction, up across the next field to find a well camouflaged stile in the field corner. Resume your previous direction half left across the next field and go through a gap in a fence immediately to the left of a tree clump which, like so many similar groups of trees in the area, shelters a small pond. Follow a right field edge out to a lane and turn left.

After about 100 yards, about 20 yards beyond a 'No footway' road sign **(6),** *turn right through a belt of scrub to a stile and then bear left, downhill, to cross a wide stream bridge. Go forward for a few yards, then left over a low sheep wire fence, where the stile has collapsed, and climb a low bank. Now head out slightly right across a field to join a tarmac access drive in the field corner. Turn right and follow this drive for over a quarter of a mile.*

At Wedd's Farm, go ahead, squeezing to the left of an outbuilding with the farmhouse on your left, walk round two sides of a tennis court to a stile, then left

Converted oasts, Old Shoyswell Manor.

round two sides of a pond and forward with more outbuildings to your left. Beyond the last building, go right through a gate and bear left, contouring along a grassy slope to reach another gate. Continue with a wood on your right and, at the end of the wood, bear half left down across grass.

A few yards short of the Limden go right through a gate and walk along the valley with the stream on your left. Walk out past another converted oast at Lymden Farm to join a road and turn left. Follow the road which climbs steadily up out of the valley. After 300 yards **(7),** *turn right along a bridleway which starts along the access to Mabb's Hill Oast and, after a few yards, continues as a hedged track, which may be muddy underfoot in places. Follow it through to another lane and turn right.*

After a little over 100 yards, at the entrance to Bardown Farm **(8),** *go left on a path which squeezes to the left of a farm area with a high wooden fence on your right. Where the fence ends, go over a stile, half right to a second stile and on for a few yards to enter a fenced downhill path.*

From this path you can enjoy a wide panoramic view southwards across the main Rother valley. Over to your left is the stumpy spire of Stonegate church.

A clear path continues through a wood and on along the right edge of a field with the wood on your right at first. From the corner of the wood, go ahead to find a stile to the left of yet another tree lined pond.

At the time of writing, as indicated by a notice and map, the area to the right of the path beyond this point is dedicated for public access under the Countryside Stewardship Scheme, offering a tour to several similar ponds.

To complete the walk, continue along a right field edge, partly along an open headland, partly between fence and ditch. In the field corner cross the railway **(9)** *and turn left beside the railway perimeter fence which you can now follow along the left edge of two fields and across a stream in a dip where you must struggle with an awkward wire gate. Continue alongside the railway through two more fields to join a road. Turn left over the railway back to the station car park.*

Walk 12

BURWASH AND THE DUDWELL VALLEY

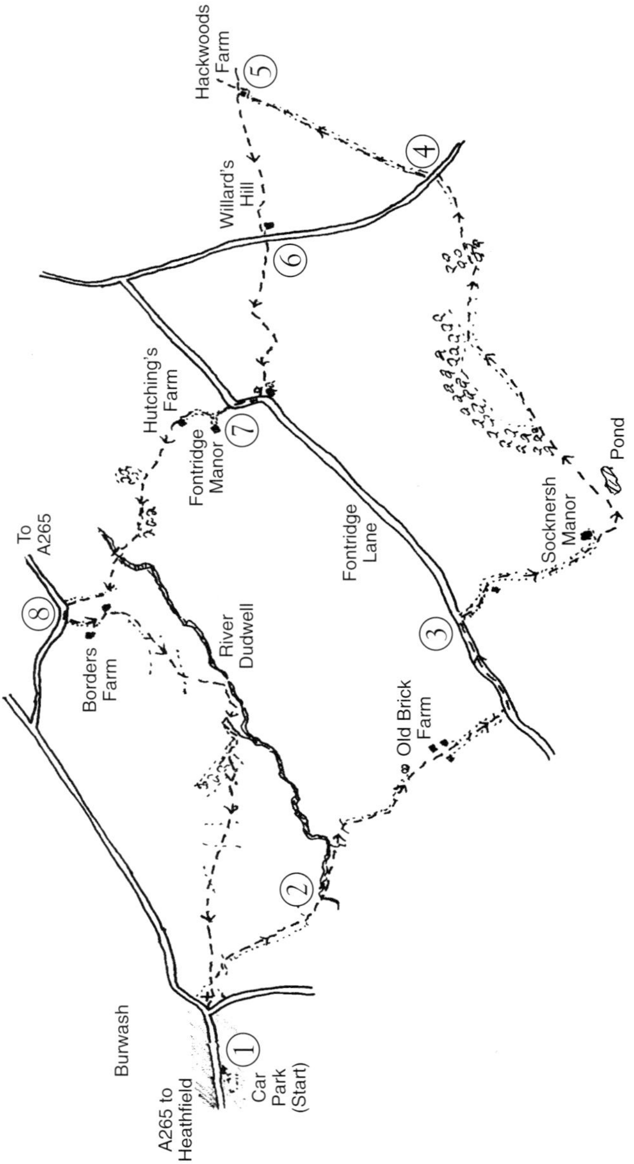

Walk 12

BURWASH AND THE DUDWELL VALLEY

Distance:	$7^1/_2$ miles
Route:	Burwash - Old Brick Farm - Socknersh Manor - Hackwoods Farm - Willard's Hill - Borders Farm - Burwash.
Map:	OS Explorer 136: The Weald
Start/Parking:	From the village of Burwash on the A265 Heathfield-to-Hurst Green road. Park in the village car park to the south of the High Street. The entrance is next to the Bear Hotel (GR 674247).
Public Transport:	Weekday bus from Uckfield, Heathfield or Etchingham Station.
Conditions:	Mostly along field paths, some showing few signs of use and therefore not always easy to follow.
Refreshments:	Pubs and tea rooms at Burwash.

The village of Burwash stands, like several Wealden settlements, high on a ridge between valleys carved by tributaries of the Rother. It owed its original prosperity to the iron-smelting industry which flourished in past centuries and this is reflected in the large number of fine old houses lining the village street. It is still a busy community with a variety of shops and several pubs. Our walk starts out along the attractive High Street, lined with pollarded lime trees, before dropping down to cross the valley of the Dudwell, the principal tributary of the Rother. It then seeks out some less used paths on the southern slopes of the valley, where navigation needs particular care, particularly beyond point 5 where you may have to contend with lush summer growth and cross field paths obscured by growing crops. Follow the route description with care, take your time to seek out the right route, have a map to hand in case you do go astray and you will be rewarded by a lovely walk through a densely patterned landscape of small fields and woods which probably hasn't altered much over hundreds of years.

THE WALK

From the car park **(1),** *turn right along the High Street as far as the church. Walk through the churchyard, skirting to the right of the church.*

The church, although largely a Victorian restoration, incorporates a Norman tower and contains a 14th Century iron grave slab, inscribed with name of a medieval ironmaster.

Keep to the upper tarmac path through the churchyard, leaving it down stone steps. After a few yards along the top edge of a meadow, just short of a recently planted memorial oak tree, fork right downhill, soon walking parallel to a hedge, a few yards away on your right. After a little over 100 yards, bear right through a gap in this hedge and drop downhill along a right field edge. In the field corner go through another gap and veer slightly left across the middle of an area of rough pasture to go through a wide hedge gap and immediately turn right to cross a footbridge over the River Dudwell **(2).**

Once over the bridge, turn left along the stream bank. After about 200 yards, go ahead across a bridge over a side stream and on across a meadow to another footbridge. Continue along a left field edge which soon veers left and begins to climb

High Street, Burwash.

View back towards Burwash from path near Old Brick Farm.

out of the valley. Pass a tree-shaded pond on your left, go left through a gate and resume your previous direction with a fence, right, to a gate and on along a drive between the buildings at Old Brick Farm and uphill to join a road (Fontridge Lane). Turn left.

After about a quarter of a mile **(3),** *turn right along the metalled drive to Socknersh Farm and Manor, signposted as a bridleway. Walk past the gateway to the manor on your left and shortly go ahead over a stile and forward with a post and rail fence on your left.*

Over to your left you now get a good view of Socknersh Manor, a fine 17th century timber-framed manor house which, like Bateman's (see walk footnote), owes its existence to the Wealden iron industry.

From the corner of the garden, go forward past a waypost and shortly veer left across two fenced culverts and on along the valley, where more posts indicate the line of the right of way. Down the hill to your right is a recently excavated ornamental lake, not yet marked on the OS map. Enter woodland through a bridle gate and follow a fenced path within the right edge of the wood. Continue between hedges and on with a hedge on your left only through two fields, climbing gently in the second field with a belt of trees to your left.

Go over a broken stile in the top field corner and veer slightly right, dropping down along a right field edge with a low tree-lined bank on your right. From the field corner a path winds through trees to a footbridge. Over the bridge, bear left through a gate and across a meadow. Shortly go left over two stiles in quick succession into woodland and immediately, where the path divides, bear right. Beyond another stile, where you

Socknersh Manor.

have a choice of three paths, yours is the one in the middle (straight on), climbing steadily. Go through a wicket gate and on in the same direction across a field to a similar gate. Continue past a small pond and a shed to join a road **(4).**

You now have a choice of two parallel access driveways opposite. Walk along the one on the right, to Hackwoods Farm. Where the drive ends in front of a gateway to a creeper covered house **(5),** *go right for a few yards, left along a narrow path, possibly overgrown, skirting to the right of the house and garden, then left again, behind the house, along a field edge.*

From the corner of the garden, head out across a field where the path may be obscured by a growing crop, go through a hedge gap and squarely out across another cultivated field. Drop down to find a hidden footbridge a few yards to the right of the bottom left field corner. Continue along a right field edge. In the field corner go right over a stile and left along a gravel drive. After 100 yards turn left up steps and along a short path laid with wood chippings out to a lane at Willard's Hill **(6).**

Go through a gap opposite to a gate and forward along the left edge of an area of neglected pasture. Go through a wide gap into the next field and veer slightly right, diverging from the hedge on your left and dropping down to pass obliquely beneath minor power lines. After another 100 yards, go right over a stile and a new footbridge in the hedge on your right and forward along a right field edge. After about 100 yards the right of way veers half left across a meadow. There is no defined path but aim a little to the left of a corner of woodland jutting out into the field from the left, to seek out a stile and a short woodland path leading to a road.

Turn right and, after less than 100 yards **(7),** *fork left along the drive to Fontridge Manor. Where the drive to the manor forks left, go ahead, and, after a few yards, in front of the gate to Hutching's Farmhouse, bear right with the main drive. Coming to farm buildings on your right and Hutching's Farmhouse on your left, go ahead through a gate and veer slightly left down across pasture. Pass to the left of a copse to a gate and bear left to drop downhill along the left edge of two fields. In the second field, go through the second gate on your left and veer slightly right across a field to another gate and right beside a right hand hedge.*

In the field corner cross the Dudwell, go through a bridle gate, then left beside the stream for 50 yards to go through a gap to the right of a gate. Now veer half right across a low-lying meadow with a large house called Borders, incorporating twin oasts, ahead. Join and follow a hedge on your right to a gate and follow a left field edge until you can go left over a footbridge in this hedge and right along a right field edge to join a lane over a stile.

Turn left and, after about 100 yards **(8),** *go left again along the concrete drive to Borders Farm. Skirt to the left of the farmyard to continue along a hedged drive until, about 100 yards short of the house, you can go right along a signed path which passes along the right edge of a garden to a gate and continues beside a right hand hedge and ditch. In the field corner, go ahead over a stile and on across a field to go through a gap a few yards to the right of a power pole. Go forward with a fence on your right but, after less than 100 yards, veer left down to a gate.*

Borders.

Go ahead for 70 yards to reach another gate but don't go through it. Instead, turn right in front of the gate to follow the Dudwell stream on your left. In the corner, go through a gate and bear half right across a field to join and follow a right hand hedge as it rounds a corner and leads you to a bridle gate into woodland. Just inside the wood go left on a faint path to a stile out of the wood. Now bear half right across pasture aiming for the left hand end of a cluster of trees surrounding a pond where you will find a stile. Head straight out across the next field, skirting to the left of another tree-shrouded pond and dropping down to a stile, soon in sight. Veer half right up across the next field, go through a gap in the next hedge and on in the same direction up across the field beyond to find a gap in the left hand hedge. Now follow a hedge on your right to a stile in the field corner and continue through a belt of trees to another stile. Head out across the next field, diverging at about 30 degrees from the hedge on your left, your next stile soon in sight. Continue through trees and along the side of the hill.

You will pass a well placed seat with a fine view to your left across the Dudwell valley.

Continue back into Burwash, retracing your outgoing route through the churchyard to the High Street.

Footnote: while in the area, if time and energy allow, be sure to visit Bateman's. About half a mile south of Burwash, this stone manor house was built by a local ironmaster in 1634 and was the home of Rudyard Kipling from 1902 until 1936. Now owned by the National Trust, it is open from April to October, Saturday to Wednesday, 11 to 6.

Walk 13

BODIAM AND SALEHURST

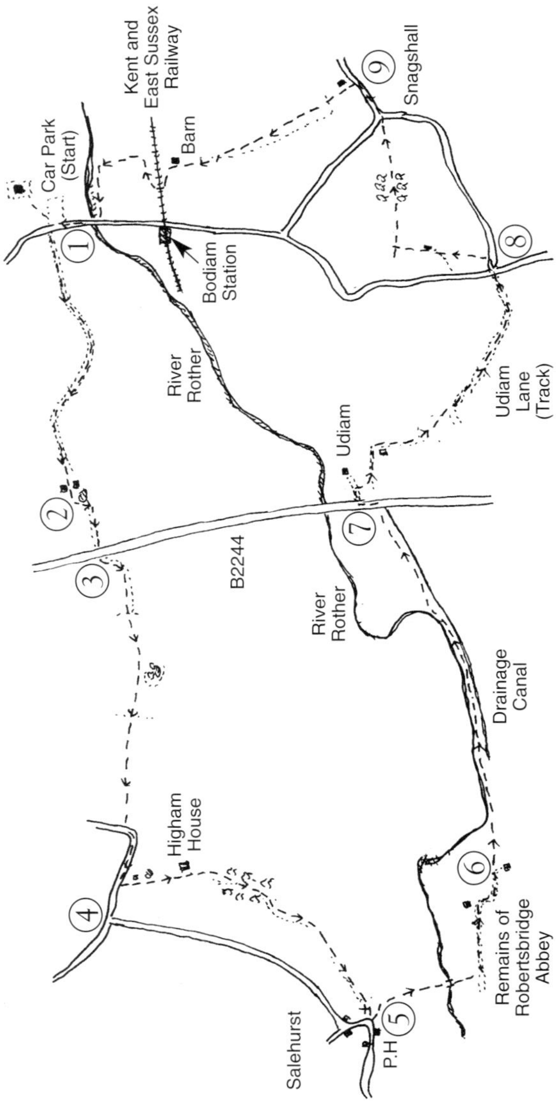

Walk 13

BODIAM AND SALEHURST

Distance:	7 miles
Route:	Bodiam Castle - Higham House - Salehurst - Robertsbridge Abbey - River Rother - Udiam - Snagshall - Bodiam Castle.
Map:	OS Explorer 136: The Weald
Start/ Parking:	From Bodiam, most easily accessible from the B2244 road about 6 miles south of Hawkhurst. Park in the large National Trust car park at Bodiam castle (£1 fee - free to NT members) at GR 784254.
Public Transport:	Occasional weekday bus service from Hawkhurst or Hastings.
Conditions:	Generally easy going, mostly on good paths or tracks.
Refreshments:	Pubs at Bodiam and Salehurst. Tea rooms at Bodiam.

This walk explores the gentle hills rising on both sides of the River Rother between Bodiam and Robertsbridge where the valley is still fairly narrow, overlooked and no doubt once guarded by Bodiam Castle at a time when the river was navigable by French marauders as far as Bodiam Bridge. Starting out to the north of the river, we climb gently before dropping down to Salehurst, once the centre of a large parish but now a peaceful isolated hamlet following expansion of the main parish settlement at Robertsbridge. A mile or so of walking beside the Rother is followed by a sharpish climb, rewarded by the best view of the day from high ground on the south side of the valley. A final descent brings us directly back to Bodiam Castle, hopefully with time and energy to spare for a tour of this superb historical site.

Although little more than a shell, Bodiam Castle appears remarkably intact when viewed from afar, a perfect realisation of the medieval castle, its foursquare walls rising directly out of the surrounding moat. It was built in the 14th century, dismantled during the civil war, and painstakingly restored in the early years of the 20th Century. It is now looked after by the National Trust and is open daily for most of the year (weekends only in mid-winter).

THE WALK

From the entrance to the car park **(1)** *turn right and, after a few yards, go left along an access drive, leaving the Castle Inn and subsequently a recreation ground on your left. Follow this drive along the valley for the best part of a mile, eventually passing some large buildings, used for light industry. About 80 yards beyond the last building* **(2),** *turn sharply back to the left between a high fence on your left and a stream on your right. A short gravel path skirts to the right of a newly constructed pond. Cross a stile and turn squarely right across a field to join the B2244 road over a stile beside a gate* **(3).**

Go over the stile opposite and bear left uphill along a left field edge. Walk round two sides of this field following a line of fine old oak trees up to a stile in the top field corner. Go straight ahead across the next field, past a tall post where you should veer slightly right, aiming for the right hand corner of a group of trees surrounding a pond. Continue in the same direction across the field to a stile in the next hedge. Head squarely out across another large field to find the next stile, and then go forward between two ponds and along a left field edge to join a lane where you should turn left.

After about 250 yards **(4),** *go left through the entrance to a house called Lake Abbot. It looks very private but you are on a public footpath. Take a straight course ahead through the garden, passing to the right of a pond to join a drive through an iron*

Bodiam Castle.

Bodiam Bridge.

gate. Continue along the drive ahead, passing to the right of Higham House. Go between brick gateposts and, after another 100 yards, go ahead, diverging to the right of the drive to a stile and on along the right edge of a grassed area.

Follow a right-handed post and rail fence until you can go right over a stile and down through a wood with a high wire mesh fence on your right. Leave the wood over a stile and follow a right field edge down, following it left and subsequently right, now heading towards the square tower of Salehurst church. At a drive, go right for five yards, then left through a gap and along a headland path. Skirt to the left of a house and garden and enter the churchyard between two massive trees.

Salehurst church is one of the biggest in rural Sussex and probably owes its size to the fact that it was taken over and enlarged by the Cistercian Abbey of Robertsbridge in the 14th century. Constructed from local sandstone, it boasts an 84 ft nave. Its greatest treasure is the 12th century 'Salamander Font,' reputedly donated to the Abbot of Robertsbridge by Richard Coeur de Lion. Just down the lane in front of the church is the Salehurst Halt pub, a reminder of the days when the railway from Tenterden to Robertsbridge passed close by.

Leave the churchyard through the main gate **(5)** *and immediately turn left and, after a few yards, left again, doubling back along a track. After a few yards keep left along a path with the churchyard at the top of the bank on your left. The path soon heads out across the valley. Cross the River Rother and continue to a T-junction with a metalled drive where you should turn left. Follow this drive past the site of Robertsbridge Abbey.*

Salehurst Church.

The remains of Robertsbridge Abbey, a Cistercian foundation of 1176, are partially visible from the drive but are not open to the public. A 13th century arch has been incorporated into a more modern house and the ruins of the Abbey refectory stand in the garden.

Follow the drive as it bears right and subsequently left. Ignore a signed bridleway to the right and shortly, where the drive bends right **(6),** *go ahead over a stile beside a gate and forward beside a post and rail fence to another stile and on along a fenced path with the raised bank of the Rother on your left. At a footpath fingerpost, turn left up steps in this bank and right on a path, overgrown and eroded in places, which follows the top of the bank with the Rother on your left and a deep drainage ditch on your right.*

About 100 yards short of a bridge over the Rother which once carried the railway across the river, fork right down the bank. Skirt to the right of a pillbox and a massive oak tree and head out along a right field edge with the drainage ditch still on your right, to reach the B2244. Turn left and, after 100 yards **(7),** *go right along the drive to Udiam. As you approach this elegant brick and tile-hung farmhouse, go right over two stiles in quick succession and left uphill along a left field edge passing to the right of a stable block with dovecotes attached at either end.*

In the field corner go over a stile and on for a few yards to a junction with a farm

River Rother.

track where you should turn right and continue uphill. Just short of a gateway, go left through a wide gap and immediately right, along a right field edge, still climbing. In the field corner go over an odd stile, topped with a 'curtain' of plastic pipes. The right of way now officially heads out across the middle of an orchard. There is no defined path and you may find it easier to walk round the right hand edge. Both routes bring you to another pipe-hung stile allowing you to join and turn left along a hedged track and follow it out to a lane.

This track is marked as Udiam Lane on the OS map and is probably an ancient highway, linking two north-south roads, still in use.

Go right, and, immediately left along Shoreham Lane, signposted to Ewhurst Green. After a few yards **(8)** *go left over a stile and head out across a field with a stunning view ahead across the Rother valley with Bodiam Castle in clear view. Go over a stile where the field boundary protrudes from the left to form a corner. Pass to the left of two sheds and continue along a gravel drive until you can turn right on a crossing path, through an orchard and on through woodland.*

A series of notices, helpfully erected by the landowner, tells us that this is an organic orchard, managed without chemicals. This ancient oak wood was destroyed about 25 years ago but the present owner is allowing it to regenerate naturally, augmented with some new oak planting.

Path beside River Rother between points 6 and 7.

Beyond the wood, head out across a field to join a road at a junction where you should go ahead, signposted to Ewhurst Green and Northiam. After about 250 yards **(9),** *turn left along a track which starts to the left of the drive to a house called Romney Lodge. Carry on in the same direction downhill across pasture, walking parallel to the fence on your left. In the bottom field corner, go left over a stile, right for a few yards to a footbridge and forward along a left field edge. Beyond a barn on your right use a stiled crossing over a railway line.*

This is part of the Kent and East Sussex Railway, which opened as late as 1900 and, in its hey-day, carried hop-pickers on the last stage of their journey to the hop fields which once dominated the valley. In 2000 the line, already restored from Tenterden to Northiam, was extended through to Bodiam and operates steam-hauled trains during the summer (Telephone 01580 765155 for more information).

Beyond the railway, turn right round two sides of a large field, then left along the raised Rother river bank out to the road, Turn right over the river back to the start.

Udiam Farmhouse.

Udiam Farmhouse and dove cotes - note doves on farmhouse roof.

Walk 14

THE ISLE OF OXNEY

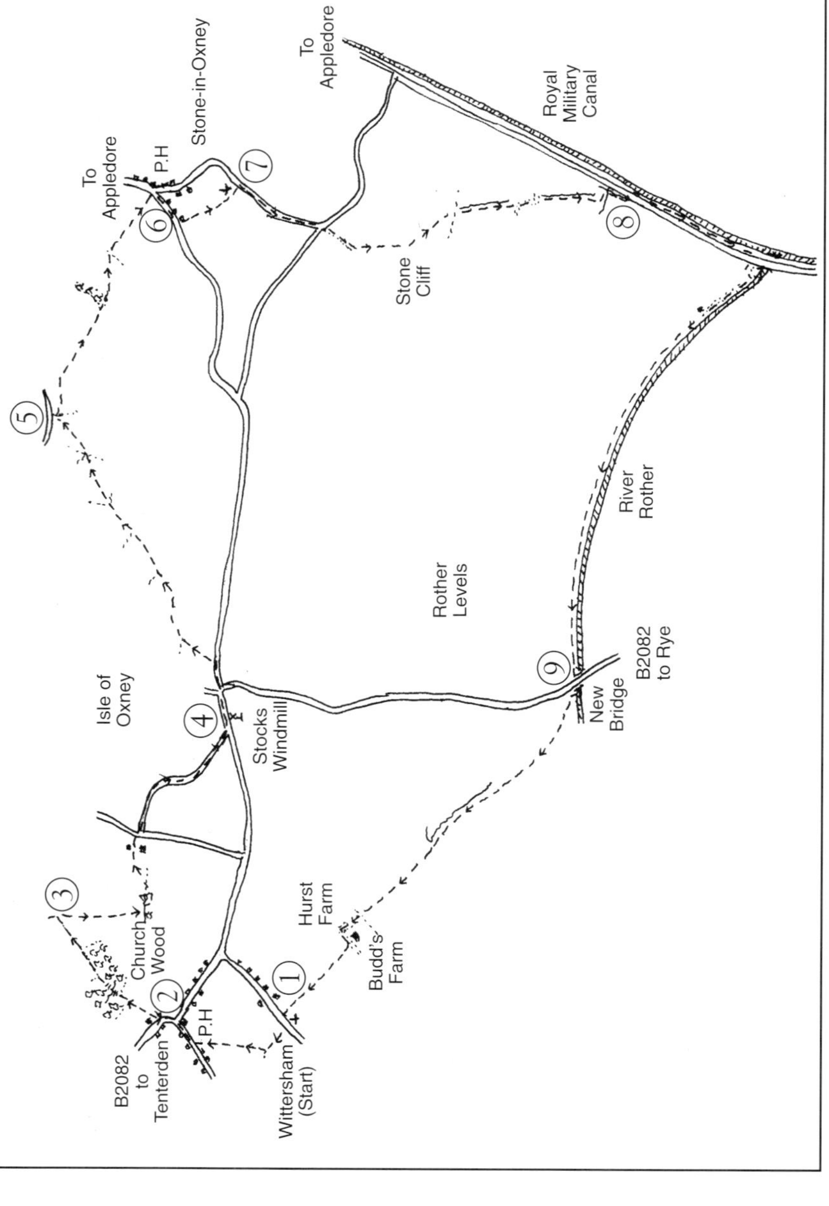

Walk 14

THE ISLE OF OXNEY

Distance:	$9^1/_2$ miles.
Route:	Wittersham Church - Church Wood - Stocks Windmill - Stone-in-Oxney - Royal Military Canal - River Rother - Hurst Farm - Wittersham.
Map:	OS Explorer 125: Romney Marsh
Start/Parking:	Wittersham on the B2082 Tenterden-to-Rye road about half way between the two towns. Roadside parking is practicable in the vicinity of the church at GR 897270.
Public Transport:	Approximately two-hourly weekday bus service from Rye or Tenterden.
Conditions:	Field, woodland and riverside paths, all in good condition, except for short sections through growing crops.
Refreshments:	Pubs at Wittersham and Stone-in-Oxney.

The 'Isle' of Oxney was true to its name at least until the Roman occupation after which the sea receded. It is still surrounded by rivers, drainage channels and reclaimed marshland. The River Rother once flowed to the north of the 'island' but was diverted to the south side in the 17th Century. The old channel still exists as the Reading Sewer and the circle of waterways is completed by the Royal Military Canal to the east and the Newmill Channel to the west.

The first half of our walk keeps to higher ground, linking the two isolated villages of Wittersham and Stone-in Oxney, both with pubs and fine sandstone churches. The descent of the steep cliff on the south side of the 'island' is the highlight of the walk, where a wide view opens out across the Rother Valley. After a short but delightful stretch beside the tree-lined Royal Military Canal, the return route includes a remote and windswept mile along or below the raised flood bank of the Rother with no shelter but offering an opportunity to enjoy big skies and open views.

THE WALK

Set out along a signed tarmac footpath which starts opposite Wittersham Church **(1).** *After about 200 yards, fork right over a stile and follow a path which winds through an orchard to enter a belt of trees. Cross a stream and stile and immediately fork right to a second stile and head out across a meadow and on between houses to join a lane. Turn right. At a road junction with the B2082 next to the Swan Inn* **(2),** *turn left.*

Just past a bus stop on the right, turn right along a wide unevenly surfaced access drive. Where this ends at a stile and gate, go ahead for a few yards to a second stile and on through woodland. Ignore the first stile on your left but after another 60 yards, go left over a second stile and drop steeply down steps to a stream and up another set of steps. A clear path continues along the left edge of Church Wood. The path angles right and left between two ponds and continues on a grassy strip between recently established hawthorn hedges.

A few yards short of a bridle gate **(3)** *go right over a stile and double sharply back on your previous course, following the direction of a waymark across a large field where a path should be apparent through any growing crop. Cross a stream in a*

Wittersham Church.

Wittersham Churchyard

wooded dip, go over a stile and turn left along a left field edge until you can go left back over the stream through a wide gap in the hedge. Now go right along a right field edge. In the corner go over a stile, then forward along the right edge of a grassy area. Skirt to the left of an outbuilding and to the right of a cottage and garden to reach a road at a junction. Follow the lane directly ahead for over a quarter of a mile out to the B2082 and turn left.

On your right is Stocks Mill, a fine old post mill, in good condition externally, which probably dates from1781. It is open to view on Sundays and Bank Holiday Mondays from May to September between 2.30 and 5 pm.

A few yards past the windmill **(4)**, *where the main road bears round to the right, go ahead, signposted to Stone and Appledore, ignoring the lane, signed to Ebony, which goes off to the left. After about 150 yards, go left over a stile and ahead across two meadows, punctuated by stiles. Once into a third field, go ahead along the right edge, passing a converted barn, a short distance away to your right. Beyond the next stile, veer slightly right to a stile beside a gate and go ahead across a field. On the other side of the field, bear left with a high hedge on your right, staying within the same field. In the field corner, sidestep to the right over a sleeper bridge, sandwiched between two stiles, and resume your previous direction with a fence on your left.*

As you proceed, a view begins to open up ahead towards Appledore on the western fringe of Romney Marsh, once the flood plain of the River Rother until its course was altered.

Stocks Windmill

In the next field, veer slightly right, diverging from the fence on your left and dropping gently down to a stile beside a gate, soon in sight. Maintain your direction across the next field, passing to the right of a field corner, jutting out from the left.

Go over two stiles in quick succession about 40 yards to the right of the far field corner (not the one in the corner leading out to a road) **(5).** *Go ahead along the left edge of a paddock with a bungalow and garden on your left. Go over a stile in the field corner and veer very slightly right across the next field to another stile. Cross a drive, go ahead along the right edge of a paddock to a stile and on across rough ground to join a track. Bear left for a few yards, then right to follow a stiled route between two paddocks and on across a large field, passing a few yards to the left of an electricity pylon. Ignore the first stile on your left, but after a few more yards, go left over a second stile into woodland.*

This tiny, but precious sliver of woodland, in a largely treeless area, is now protected in the hands of the Woodland Trust.

A few yards inside the wood, go right to a stile. From the stile a trodden path goes ahead along a headland but you should veer half left across an area of pasture, heading for the left end of a row of pollarded poplar trees. Go through a wide gap in the far left field corner and ahead along a right field edge with a ditch and hedge on your right. Go through a gap into the next field and veer slightly right, as indicated by a waymark, to reach the road at Stone-in-Oxney, opposite the Crown Inn **(6).**

Turn right along the road. After about 200 yards, go left along a hedged path which squeezes to the right of a cottage and winds through an area of scrubby woodland to a gate and on with a post and rail fence to the left. Beyond a stile, go straight ahead across an undulating field, dipping to cross a stream and climbing towards Stone-in Oxney church. Walk through the churchyard and out to a lane **(7).**

The present church, a sturdy sandstone building, replaced a previous structure, destroyed by fire in 1464. Inside, beneath the tower, you can seek out a much-battered Roman Altar with the just discernible carving of a bull (the one slain by Mithras) on each side.

Turn right along the lane. At a road junction, go straight ahead over a stile and forward along a right field edge to another stile in the field corner and half left down across two fields with a stile between them.

From this path, as it descends sharply down the grassy southern slope of the Isle of Oxney, a wide view opens out southwards across the Rother valley.

Beyond a gate, the path continues down a grassy shelf, through a gate and on in the same direction obliquely down the undulating slope to a stile and then forward with ditch on your right out on to the drained marshland. Divert a few yards right to a culvert over a wide side ditch, and continue along the right bank of a more substantial drainage channel. Join and go ahead along a farm track. Where this track turns away to the left, next to a small hut, keep right on a path beside another minor waterway until, when confronted by a deeper channel you can turn left beside it, and shortly right with another waterway on your left. Follow this until you can go left over a bridge out to a road **(8).** *Cross the road, go over the stile, opposite, and turn right along the raised bank of the Royal Military Canal.*

Stone-in-Oxney Church.

View from path near Stone-in-Oxney Church.

This is a beautiful tree-lined section of the canal, built in 1807 as part of the defence system constructed to repel a threatened Napoleonic invasion.

After a little over a quarter of a mile beside the canal, rejoin the road, go left for a few yards, then right along a track which you can follow round to the left and out to join the Rother river bank. Turn right and follow the river for over a mile. Cross the B2082 **(9),** *go over two stiles, opposite and, immediately, turn right to a third stile walking squarely away from the river. Now veer half left across a large field, where a path is usually trodden through any growing crop. On the other side of the field, cross a bridge and continue with a ditch on your right, following it as it curves gently left. Where this ditch turns sharply away to the right, go ahead across a field (there is no defined path), climbing gently at first and aiming for a house, just visible through trees on the skyline. On the other side of the field, go over a stile and contour along a grassy slope. After about 100 yards, just past a gap in the hedge on your left, which should be ignored, go left over a half-hidden stile and climb, half right up a grassy slope.*

Go through a bridle gate, across the drive to Budds House and forward across grass to join and follow another drive. Follow this drive round to the left and ahead with a house and garden on your left. After 100 yards turn right along a grassy track walking beneath minor power lines with Wittersham Church in view ahead. The track becomes a gravel drive past two large new houses. Shortly fork left through a bridle gate, cross a drive, go through another gate and continue beside Wittersham churchyard out to a road within yards of the start.

Royal Military Canal.

Walk 15

SEDLESCOMBE AND BATTLE

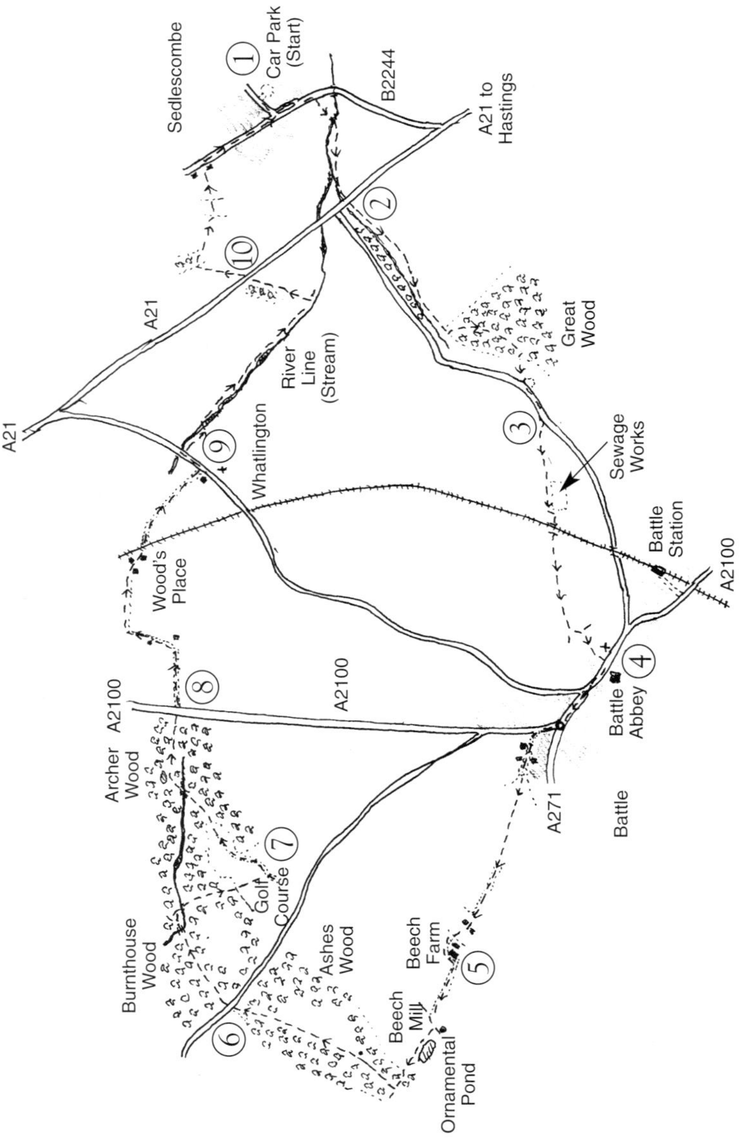

Walk 15

SEDLESCOMBE AND BATTLE

Distance:	$10^1/_2$ miles
Route:	Sedlescombe - Great Wood - Battle -Beech Farm - Ashes Wood - Burnthouse Wood - Archer Wood - Wood's Place - Whatlington - River Line - Sedlescombe.
Map:	OS Explorer 124: Battle and Hastings
Start/Parking:	From Sedlescombe, signposted from the A21 along the B2244 about 6 miles north of Hastings. Park in the village car park, signposted to the east of the village street at GR 782180.
Public Transport:	Occasional weekday bus service from Hastings.
Conditions:	A mix of field, riverbank and woodland paths and tracks, moderately hilly but with no severe or prolonged gradients.
Refreshments:	Pubs and tea rooms at Sedlescombe and Battle.

The main focus of this walk is Battle, a substantial small town which has grown up around the site of what was, perhaps, the most important event in English history, the Battle of Hastings, where William the Conqueror defeated King Harold in 1066. Reached about an hour and a half into the walk, it offers a chance for rest and refreshment as well as an opportunity to visit the abbey, founded by William to commemorate his victory. It is run by English Heritage and open daily throughout the year. The admission price includes an audio tour of the battle site.

Our starting and finishing point is the charming village of Sedlescombe, frequent winner of best-kept village competitions. We set out and return along two of the intimate river valleys formed by the main feeder streams of the River

Brede. In between, we climb across a sandstone ridge separating the two valleys, passing through mixed woodland as well as more open country with extensive views. It all adds up to one of the most varied and beautiful as well one of the longest walks in this book. Allow yourself a full day for it, particularly if you are planning to explore Battle in any depth.

THE WALK

From Sedlescombe village car park **(1)**, *return to the main road through the village and turn left downhill beside the village green, past the Queen's Head pub and the post office. At the bottom of the hill, just past the Bridge Garage on your right, turn right along a gravel drive, passing to the right of a tennis court and recreation ground. Cross a stream and immediately turn right along the right edge of a low-lying meadow with a stream nearby on your right.*

Cross the A21 **(2)** *and follow the footpath, opposite, which continues with the stream along the valley. At the far end of a long field go over a stile and along an enclosed path. At a T-junction with a heavily used crossing path, turn left and shortly go through a gap beside a gate into Great Wood and forward on a wide woodland track. After a little over a quarter of a mile, soon after the edge of the wood becomes visible through trees on your right, look out for a narrow path on the right which leads, after a few yards, to a stile beside a gate at the edge of the wood.*

Cross rough pasture, go over a stream and another stile beside a gate. Cross the

Queen's Head Pub and village green, Sedlescombe.

The path along the valley from Sedlescombe.

corner of the next field and continue in the same direction across the field beyond to join a road next to a forestry car park. Turn left beside the road and, after 150 yards **(3),** *go right along a short access track, then left over a stile to head out across a field where a path should be trodden out if it is under cultivation. From a stile on the other side of this field, an enclosed path continues, soon skirting to the right of a sewage treatment works.*

At the far corner of this area, turn left along a track for five yards only before going right along a woodland path which tunnels beneath the railway to a gate. Continue with a stream on your left to a gap in the next hedge and on along the valley, now beside a right hand hedge. Maintain direction across two more fields to a stile and footbridge from which a path winds on for a short distance to join a roughly metalled drive where you should turn left. After less than 100 yards, go left again over the remains of a stile and across pasture to a footbridge. Now climb steeply across pasture, aiming a little to the right of the square tower of St. Mary's Church, Battle on the skyline. Beyond a stile, a short path leads out to Battle High Street **(4).**

The entrance to Battle Abbey is now only a few yards away on the other side of the High Street. Between the end of March and the end of September it is open from 10 to 6, shorter hours in winter. It is closed only for three days over Christmas and on New Year's Day. (Telephone 01424 773792 for more information).

The path up towards Beech Farm.

Turn right and walk along the full length of the High Street. At a roundabout, fork right along the A2100 and after 100 yards, fork left along a side road which passes a residential development and continues through a rather down-at-heel light industrial area. Where the tarmac ends and you have a choice of two routes ahead, fork right along the gravel drive to a house called Kelklands. Beyond the house the drive narrows to a path, tunnelling between banks to emerge at a field corner with a sudden sweeping view ahead across open countryside.

Head out across the centre of a field, dropping down along a fine descending ridge. At the bottom of the hill, go over a newish footbridge and climb steadily with a hedge on your right. After 350 yards, go obliquely across a drive and through a gate labelled 'footpath'. A fenced path squeezes between two cottage gardens. Continue in the same direction across a paddock to a gap in the next hedge where a plank bridge takes you across a ditch. Go forward, skirting to the right of the buildings of Beech Farm. In the field corner go left over a stile and behind a row of barns. After 50 yards go right, shortly bearing round to the left beside a high wooden wall to join a concrete drive where you should turn right **(5).**

The drive soon loses its hard surface and becomes a wide, hedged grassy track. Where this track ends, go ahead with a hedge only on your right. In the field corner, cross a stile and, after a few yards, fork left, downhill along a narrow path. After

The view back towards Battle from path approaching Beech Farm.

another 100 yards or so, turn right over a stile and along a wide fenced grassy strip with a large ornamental lake away to your left. Beyond another stile go forward along a narrow path through a stand of conifers. Keep left at a Y-junction and, at a crossing path, where there is a four-armed fingerpost, turn right and head north through Ashes Wood.

Look out for an old milestone, to the right of the path, with the inscription '55 miles from London, 2 miles to Ashburnham Place'.

Follow this rather grand avenue, lined with beech and occasional oak, for over half a mile and out via a short length of access drive to a road **(6).** *Your next path starts over a stile opposite and follows another woodland path which drops gently downhill. Shortly after crossing a stream in a charming woodland dell, fork right at a Y-junction. Where the path divides again, keep right, descending to re-cross the stream. Keep right over the remnants of a stile, cross another stream and climb fairly steeply. After leaving the wood, go ahead across a golf course, descending to go through a gap in a dip and climbing, veering slightly right. Pass to the left of a raised golf green and, after a few yards* **(7),** *join and turn sharply back to the left, dropping down along a sunken tree-lined path.*

At the bottom of the hill, bear right along the right hand edge of another segment of the golf course. At the far end of this playing area, go ahead along a wide woodland

Pond near Beech Hill.

track, across a newish bridle bridge. After passing a secluded pond, bear right with the main track and follow it out to the A2100 **(8).** *Cross the road and follow the drive, opposite. As you approach a large house (Woodsdale), ignore a concrete drive which forks left. Shortly, just before reaching the brick gateway to the house, fork left through a gate, pass between the house on your right and an outbuilding on your left and immediately, turn left along a dirt track. At a junction, bear right on a path which skirts to the right of a circular wooden structure and a derelict barn and continues ahead between overgrown hedges. After a little over 100 yards, turn right through a gap and follow a headland path along a right field edge. It becomes an unmade access drive which passes a number of houses and continues over the railway and on for a quarter of a mile to reach the road at Whatlington past a garden notable for some elaborate topiary* **(9).**

Access to the small isolated church is about 100 yards to the right along the road. It occupies a pleasant raised site, set back from the road to the left. In the churchyard is the grave of Malcolm Muggeridge, a well-known media pundit in the 1970s and 1980s.

To complete the walk, go left along the road from point 9 and, just short of a brick bridge over the River Line, turn right and follow this stream along the valley, on your left at first, then, beyond a bridge over the river, along the lower edge of a vineyard with the stream on your right. Follow the River Line along the valley for over half a mile through alternating woods and fields until, at a four-arm fingerpost you can turn squarely left across a field to a footbridge and up along the right edge of a block of woodland on your left to join the A21 **(10).**

Go through the bridle gate opposite and veer half left up across a large field. Cross an area used as an airstrip to a gate, double back through a second gate and go forward over a stile. Drop downhill along an enclosed path along the right edge of a wood. Where the enclosed path ends, veer half right across the valley floor to a gate, cross a stream and climb across a field to a stile, in sight, and on across a second field. Go through a gate and continue in the same direction across the field beyond to find two stiles immediately to the left of a bungalow, providing access out to the B2244. Turn right and walk back into Sedlescombe.

The path beyond point 10.

Walk 16

HASTINGS COUNTRY PARK AND GUESTLING

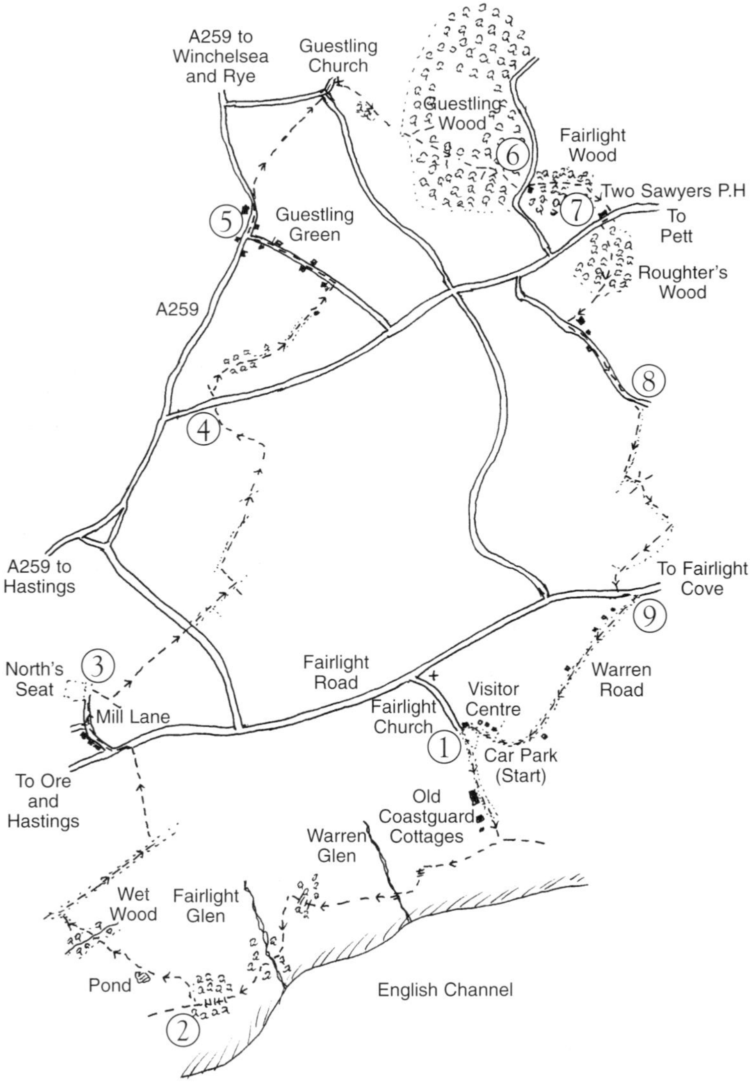

Walk 16

HASTINGS COUNTRY PARK AND GUESTLING

Distance:	$7^1/_2$ miles
Route:	Fairlight (Visitor Centre car park) - Warren Glen - Fairlight Glen - Wet Wood - North's Seat - Guestling Green - Guestling Church - Guestling Wood - Fairlight Wood - Roughter's Wood - Rosemary Lane - Warren Road - Fairlight.
Map:	OS Explore 124: Hastings and Bexhill
Start/Parking:	From the eastern end of Hastings, follow the Fairlight Road. The car park is signposted on the seaward side of the road, along Coastguard Lane. Park in the second of two car parks along the lane at GR 860116, next to a small Visitor Centre.
Public Transport:	Hourly weekday bus service to Guestling Green (two hourly on Sunday), joining the walk at point 5.
Conditions:	A hilly and fairly strenuous walk: along good paths within the Hastings Country Park. Inland, the paths are less used and tend to become overgrown, particularly in late summer.
Refreshments:	The Two Sawyers pub at point 7.

Between Hastings and Fairlight Cove the hills and ridges of the High Weald meet the sea to form a ragged line of, geologically unique, crumbling sandstone cliffs. Through this area, small streams funnel down to the sea, forming a series of sheltered glens, clothed in a patchwork of gorse, bracken and scrubby woodland. Much of the area is well protected and managed as the 640-acre Hastings Country Park.

Our walk starts by taking a switchback route along the coast within the Country Park, crossing two of the glens before heading inland up to North's

Seat, a viewpoint overlooking Hastings, and then dropping down again to Guestling Green, where navigation requires some care as the paths are little used and occasionally overgrown. The return route winds through Guestling Wood and passes the Two Sawyers Pub, a welcome refreshment stop about two-thirds of the way round the walk.

Suitably rejuvenated, you will make short work of the final climb back up to Fairlight.

THE WALK

From the car park **(1)** *start the walk by heading for the sea along the metalled access road to the coastguard station. Pass to the left of the old coastguard cottages and walk down almost to the edge of the cliff. Turn right through a swing gate, passing a solid wooden bollard, numbered 14, indicating the coast path. The path soon begins a steady descent into Warren Glen. At a path junction, turn left dropping down a steep flight of steps. Ignore a path off to the right at the bottom of the steps, continuing down to a stream at the bottom of the glen and climb steeply, signposted on another bollard to Fairlight Glen ½ mile. At the top of the first steep ascent, go straight over a crossing path and, shortly, at another bollard, go ahead up more steps through woodland.*

The path crosses high open ground before dropping steeply down again. At a T-junction by the next bollard, turn left towards the sea, dropping down to cross another

Warren Glen.

The path down to Fairlight Glen.

stream at the bottom of Fairlight Glen.

Until recently, it was possible to get down to the beach from this point, the only access down to sea level within the country park. Sadly the path is currently closed, due to cliff erosion.

Go forward for a few yards to another bollard where you should turn left with the main path which soon climbs steeply up out of the glen, where another long flight of steps takes you up through woodland. Where the path leaves the wood beside another bollard **(2)**, *turn right to walk away from the sea. A few yards past a swing gate go forward across a wooden causeway with a small pond on your left.*

From this point you get a good view back along the coast to the coastguard cottages near the start of the walk and, beyond, the distant buildings of Dungeness Power Station. Over to the left, a view has opened up across Hastings to the line of the Downs beyond Eastbourne.

The path crosses high open ground and enters woodland. At a T-junction, a few yards inside the wood turn right, now on a substantial track which dips to cross a stream and climbs again. Just past a Hastings Country Park information notice and map, join and follow the access drive from a house and, after a few yards, at a junction with another drive, turn right, past a notice 'Private Road to Fairlight Place'. Take the second waymarked path on the left, signposted to North's Seat 1/2 mile. Follow this enclosed, somewhat overgrown path through to the Fairlight Road, go left

Fairlight Glen.

for a few yards, then fork right along Mill Lane which you can now follow for 250 yards up to North's Seat **(3).**

The viewpoint indicator and picnic area, worth the short detour, are now a few yards to the left. North's Seat (or North Seat as it is incorrectly labelled on the OS map) is named after Frederic North, an MP and one time Mayor of Hastings.

To continue the walk, on reaching the North's Seat entrance notice, go right through a swing gate and along a path, signposted to Fairlight Road Picnic Site. After 100 yards, go left between staggered railings, cross an equestrian track, go over the stile opposite and forward along a path between widely spaced fences, with a glorious view eastwards and northwards into the Weald. Cross a road to a stile and continue downhill with a wood on your right.

When you come to a stile on your right, don't cross it. Instead, turn left with your back to the stile and head squarely out across a field. On the other side of the field, turn right along the left field edge. After about 300 yards, go left through a gap in the hedge on your left, and head half right across a field, passing beneath power lines a few yards to the left of a power pole. A waypost indicates the start of a path down through a wood. Cross two streams and climb for a few yards out into a field and then go left along the left edge of this hay meadow.

After 50 paces, go left across a culvert within a belt of trees and on across a field corner to a stile beside a gate. Now go forward along a narrow overgrown path to join a metalled drive. Go right between houses and out into a field and turn left along the left field edge. In the field corner go ahead along a short enclosed path out to join a road **(4).**

Your next path, signposted to Hastings Youth Hostel, starts opposite. After a few yards along this path, go right over a stile and walk between fences to the next stile leading into a wood. Follow a path, a bit vague in places, through the wood, leave the wood over another stile and follow a right field edge for a few yards to go over a stile or the hunt jump alongside it. Now bear left downhill along a left field edge. Go over a stile between a gate and another hunt jump and forward on a grassy path between widely spaced fences. Beyond a short avenue of beech trees, go over wooden railings to the right of a gate. Another narrow path between fence and hedge takes you out to a road (Chapel Lane). Turn left through the little settlement of Guestling Green. At the A259 **(5),** *go right beside the main road.*

Guestling Church.

The pub, marked with a blue tankard on the Explorer map at this point, is The Hope Inn. No hope of a drink at present, alas, as it is closed and boarded up.

Shortly, when opposite a school on the left, go right through a wide gap in the hedge and left on a trodden path which soon heads out across a field, aiming directly towards the squat spire of Guestling Church. Follow this path through two fields to join a lane where you should turn left to reach the church.

The church, occupying an isolated position, originates from the 12th to 14th centuries, though it was heavily restored after a fire in 1890. The tower, which survived the conflagration, dates from about 1100.

Enter the churchyard through the lych gate and skirt to the right of the church to find a swing gate. Once through the gate, bear half right along an unfenced grassy track which passes squarely beneath power lines and skirts to the left of a block of woodland. Continue across a field to enter Guestling Wood.

Guestling Wood is one of the larger local areas of ancient woodland (over 50 acres) owned and managed by the Woodland Trust, and open for public access along a complicated network of paths.

Two Sawyers Pub.

Ignore a left fork a few yards inside the wood. Where the waymarked 1066 Hastings Walk forks right, keep straight on along a clear track. Where the path divides again by a manhole cover, fork right and continue out to a lane through a swing gate **(6).** *Your next path starts opposite, skirting to the left of a house and garden and on through a wood. Leave the wood over a footbridge and go half right across a meadow to a stile and out to join a road. Turn right.*

The Two Sawyers pub, on the right, provides a welcome refreshment stop, with good food and beer, including real ales brewed next door to the pub in the Old Forge micro-brewery.

Just past the pub **(7),** *turn left along a signed path, narrow and enclosed at first, then down through Roughter's Wood. Leave the wood over a stile and go ahead, skirting to the right of a farm complex to join a lane (Rosemary Lane). Turn left to follow this lane past several attractive old thatched cottages. Ignore the first signed path to the right which starts over a footbridge. After another 200 yards along the lane* **(8),** *go right though a wide hedge gap and bear left round a left field edge.*

After about 300 yards, go left over a sleeper bridge and forward along a right field edge. After less than 100 yards go right over a stile where there is a sign indicating that five rights of way converge at this point. Once over the stile, go half left across a field corner to go through a wide hedge gap and then bear right to climb gently along a right field edge. After a little over 100 yards, go right over a stile beside a gate and steadily uphill, walking a straight line roughly parallel to the more meandering left field edge, to find steps up to a gate at the top end of the field.

Now bear left along a left field edge out to join the Fairlight Road over a stile. Turn left along the road for a few yards only before turning sharply back to the right along Warren Road **(9).** *Follow this road, for much of the way no more than an unmade access to a number of properties, for over half a mile back to the car park and the start.*

The Visitor Centre, next to the car park, contains displays demonstrating the geology and history of the Country Park. It is open during the summer months on weekend afternoons.

Walk 17

HIGH HURSTWOOD AND CROWBOROUGH COMMON

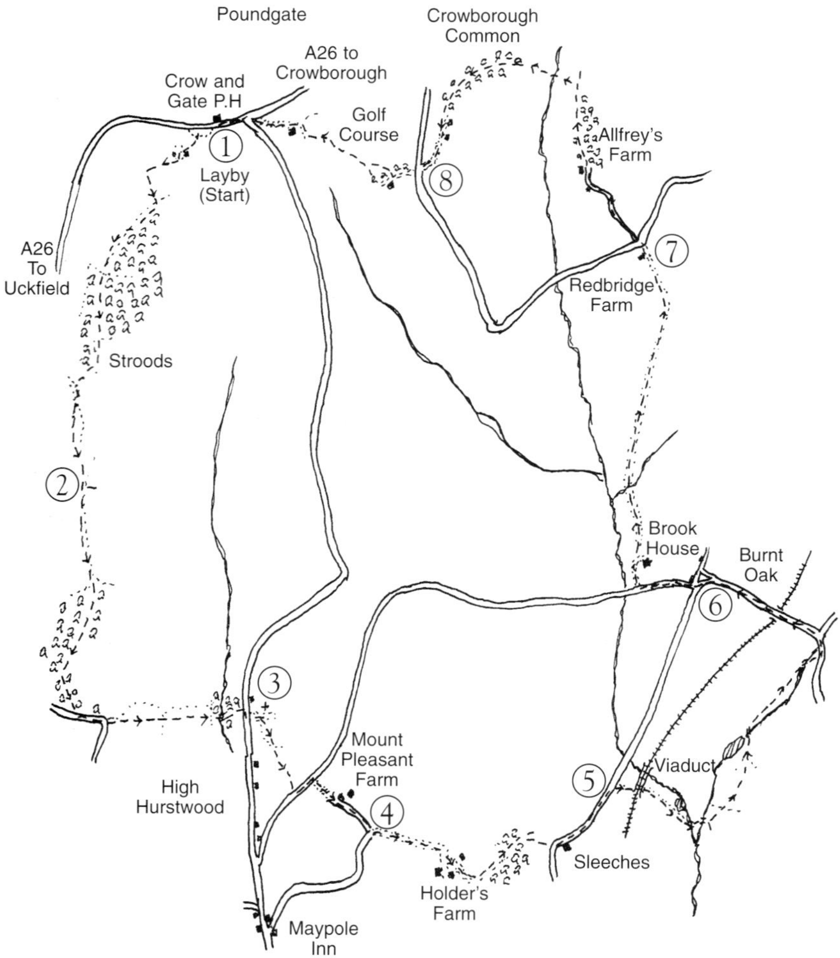

Walk 17

HIGH HURSTWOOD AND CROWBOROUGH COMMON

Distance:	$7^1/_2$ miles
Route:	Poundgate - High Hurstwood - Sleeches - Fordbrook - Brook House - Redbridge Farm - Allfrey's Farm - Crowborough Common - Poundgate.
Map:	OS Explorer 135: Ashdown Forest
Start/Parking:	In a lay-by almost opposite the Crow and Gate pub at Poundgate on the A26 about $1^1/_2$ miles south-west of Crowborough. (GR 494288)
Public Transport:	Bus from Tunbridge Wells, Lewes or Brighton (hourly on weekdays, two-hourly on Sundays).
Conditions:	Field and woodland paths, some little used, possibly overgrown and occasionally difficult to follow. Fairly hilly.
Refreshments:	Crow and Gate pub at start/finish. Maypole Inn at High Hurstwood, a quarter of a mile off the route from point 4.

To the south of Crowborough, on high ground to the east of Ashdown Forest, the land begins to drop away to the south in the form of a series of low ridges, divided by small streams flowing southwards and gathering to form the River Uck, a tributary of the Ouse. It is an intimate landscape of small fields and woods interspersed with patches of heathy bracken, reminding us that the soil underfoot is similar to the acidic sandy loam of Ashdown Forest.

Our walk picks a route through this surprisingly remote area. Although the footpath network is reasonably generous, route finding requires some care, particularly in late summer when some of these little-used paths can become overgrown. After dropping down to the scattered community of High Hurstwood, the walk turns north, using an ancient trackway beyond Brook House. The last mile crosses Crowborugh Common, partly wood and patchy heathland, partly golf course, where particular care is needed to pick out the correct route of the right of way as it crosses the playing area.

THE WALK

Start the walk through a bridle gate at the back of the lay-by **(1)** *behind a telephone box.*

A waymark on the gate indicates that you are on the Vanguard Way. This is a long distance walkers' path from East Croydon to the coast at Seaford and we shall be sampling two sections of this route on our circuit.

Cross a meadow to join a drive over a stile built into a fixed gate. Go ahead along the drive, passing between two houses to find the next stile to the right of a gate. Bear half right across a meadow to the next stile, to the right of a cattle trough and go ahead with a hedge on your right.

From this path a superb view opens out southwards across the Low Weald to the distant South Downs.

After about 100 yards beside the hedge, at a finger post, turn left across the field to enter woodland over another stile built into a gate. A path winds through the wood to a stile and then continues along a field edge with the wood on your left. In the field corner cross a stile and continue through the wood. Leave the wood, pass to the left of a house and continue with a fine plantation of mature beech trees on your right.

Shortly, at a finger post, fork right through the trees. Join a concrete drive, turn left for 15 yards and then fork right across parkland where the right of way is marked by a series of wayposts. Where the Vanguard Way goes off to the left up steps in a bank **(2),** *you should go ahead along the foot of the bank to a stile and on through a wood for a little over a quarter of a mile to join and bear left along a lane.*

After less than 200 yards, where the lane curves round to the right, go left over a stile. Follow a left hand holly hedge for a few yards and then, without change of direction, go ahead, dropping gently down across two fields with a stile between them, in the second field walking parallel to a line of four isolated oak trees. Go over a stile and follow a woodland path across a stream and out to the road at High Hurstwood **(3).** *Turn right and almost immediately left along a road, signed to the church.*

High Hurstwood church is a Victorian structure - a bit of a hotch-potch but an agreeable one, incorporating an open belfry and a solid clock tower.

Just short of the church, go right through a kissing gate and follow a trodden grassy path which runs roughly parallel to the zigzagging right-hand field edge to reach another kissing gate. A narrow path tunnels through scrub to a third gate and then heads squarely up across rough pasture to join a lane through a fourth and similar gate. Turn left and, after less than 100 paces, go right along a hedged track which becomes a

The path between points 1 and 2.

concrete access drive which you can follow to a T-junction with a lane **(4).**

For the Maypole Inn, go right along the lane for about a quarter of a mile, returning the same way.

To continue the walk, turn left at point 4, along a rough track. After about 350 yards, fork left along the drive to a house called Ironcastle and, after 40 yards, fork right over a stile beside a gate to follow a narrow overgrown path through scrubby woodland. Join a rough track on a bend and go ahead. After 40 yards, fork left across a stream, go through a gate and climb gently along a right field edge. In the field corner, go over a stile beside a gate and follow a narrow path within the right edge of woodland. After a little over 100 yards within the wood, go right over a stile and follow a left field edge to another stile. The path now squeezes to the right of a large shed to a junction with a gravel drive where you should turn right out to a lane.

Turn left along the lane and, after 350 yards **(5),** *go right over a stile beside a gate and follow a right-hand fence to pass under an impressive brick viaduct which carries the Uckfield-to-Tunbridge Wells railway line. Once under the viaduct, go forward walking beside a left-hand fence with a landscaped area and pond over to your left, not yet marked on OS maps. The fence leads you to a footbridge in a wooded dip. Go ahead for 50 yards to cross a second, substantial, footbridge.*

A fingerpost now offers you a choice of routes. Ignoring the stile on your right, continue with a hedge on your right. Shortly, in the field corner, go over a stile where waymarks, once again, offer a choice of routes. Fork half left up across pasture where there is no obvious path. Seek out twin stiles, hidden in a hedge about 100 yards down from the top left field corner. Head almost squarely out across the next field to find a stile beside a gate at the far end.

Go ahead for a few yards, join a gravel track and, almost immediately, at a waypost, fork left along a grassy path. A track continues through a wood and across a bridge at the head of a large pond, once again not marked on OS maps. After a few more yards, where the track bears away to your left, go ahead along the right hand edge of a low-lying meadow with a stream hidden behind scrub on your right. In the field corner go over a stile, across a footbridge, out through a thicket to join a road and turn left.

After 150 yards, turn left along Fordbrook Hill and after another quarter of a mile, at a place marked on the map as Burnt Oak **(6),** *fork left. Shortly, at a cross roads, go ahead along Burnt Oak Road. After another 250 yards, go right along the drive to Brook House, lined by ornamental trees and shrubs. Where the drive bends right up to the house, you should fork left along a grassy path which passes to the left of an*

High Hurstwood Church.

annexe. Follow this tree-lined track northwards for the best part of a mile, climbing gently and ignoring a signed path off to the left. The track is muddy in places and obstructed by fallen timber here and there but there is always a way through, either in the hollow way or along the bank to the right.

Where you finally come out into the open, skirt to the left of a small pond and continue up along the right edge of two fields. Pass to the left of a shed, go through a gate and follow a hedged track out to a road **(7).** *Turn left and, almost immediately, right along Allfreys Lane. Soon after passing Allfrey's Farm the road ends but continues as a dirt track through woodland, soggy underfoot in places but with a drier parallel alternative path within woodland to the right.*

A few yards short of the point where the track comes out on to a golf course, turn left along a waymarked path which drops down through a wooded strip and continues along the left edge of another part of the golf course. Join a track which drops down through a deep gully, running to the left of a higher bridge, for golfers only, over to your right. On the other side of the gully, as the track comes out on to the golf course again, go left into woodland. A path now winds through a mixture of woodland and patchy bracken, along the southern edge of Crowborough Common, well insulated from the golf course which has now swallowed up much of the common. The path eventually comes out on to a drive where you should bear right and follow it past houses and out to a lane **(8).**

Continue along the track opposite. The next section requires some care to pick out the correct route. After a few yards, at a waypost, fork right through a belt of woodland. The correct route is overgrown but you can follow a fairly direct path through the trees and out on to the golf course next to a tee. Turn left along the edge of the golf course for a few yards to find another waypost where the path officially comes out of the wood. From this point head out half left across the golf course, diverging at about 20 degrees from the wood on your left and passing a few yards to the right of the 8th Tee where you should be able to spot the next waypost, to the left of a clump of fir trees. Follow the direction of an arrow on this post through a belt of woodland and out on to a golf fairway. Go half left across the fairway and then bear left beside a thin belt of fir trees on a trodden path which skirts to the left of a green to reach the top left corner of the golf course. A narrow path continues with a high brick wall on your left at first, bringing you out to the A26 at its junction with Chillies Lane. Bear left beside the main road, past the Crow and Gate pub and back to the start.

Walk 18

HERSTMONCEUX

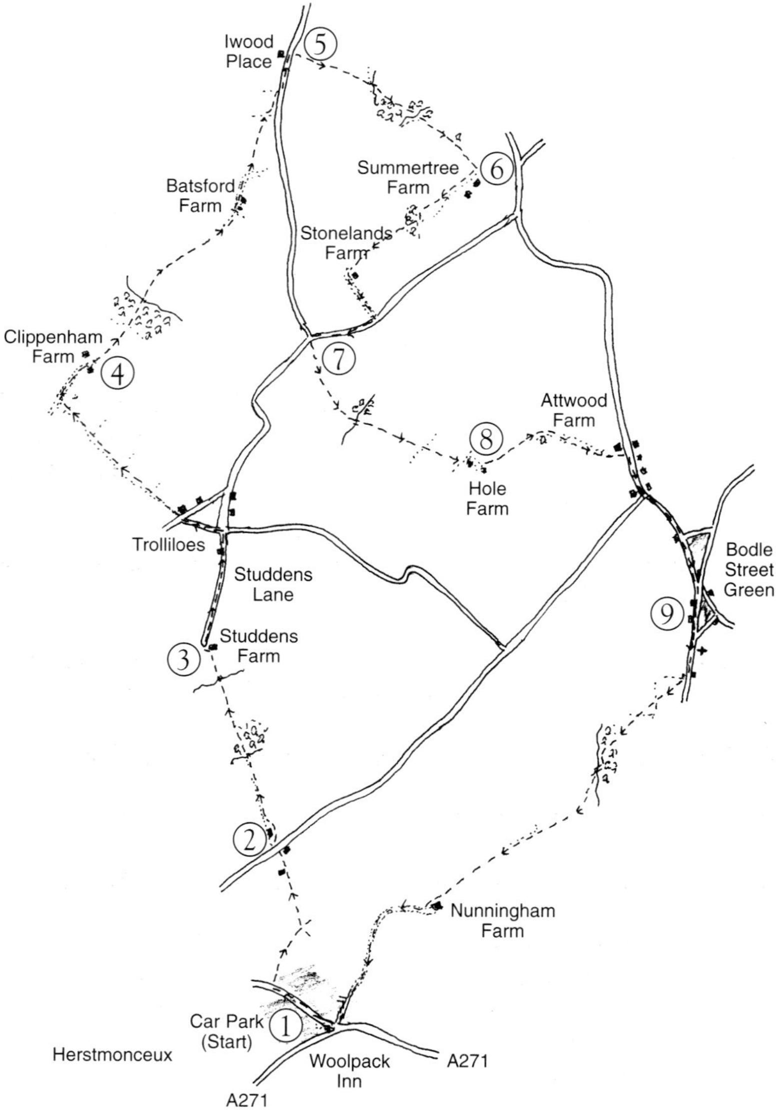

Walk 18

HERSTMONCEUX

Distance:	8 miles
Route:	Herstmonceux - Studdens Farm - Trolliloes - Clippenham Farm - Batsford Farm - Iwood Place - Summertree Farm - Stonelands Farm - Hole Farm - Attwood Farm - Bodle Street Green - Nunningham Farm - Herstmonceux.
Map:	OS Explorer 124: Hastings and Bexhill.
Start/Parking:	At Herstmonceux on the A271 Hailsham-to-Battle road. Park in the free public car park behind the Woolpack Inn in the centre of the village at GR 634126.
Public Transport:	Hourly weekday bus to Herstmonceux from Eastbourne or Hastings.
Conditions:	Mostly along little used field paths with some poor stiles and difficult gates. May be overgrown.
Refreshments:	Pubs at Herstmonceux and Bodle Street Green.

Starting from Herstmonceux on the southern edge of the High Weald and only a few feet above the Pevensey Levels which spread out to the south of the village, this walk heads northwards, gradually gaining height as it meanders across low undulating hills. It passes through a thinly populated intimate landscape of modest scale farms, small fields and tiny streams, often shaded by narrow strips of woodland.

A word of warning - the paths through this remote area are little used. Shaky stiles, awkward gates and sporadic waymarking make this a fairly adventurous walk where route finding is something of a challenge. Have a map to hand, follow the detailed directions with care and, particularly in late summer, wear leg-protecting clothing and take a stick to beat down the undergrowth which tends to encroach on the path, notably through the wood between Summertree Farm and Stonelands Farm and beyond point 8. But don't be put off. Take your time and you will be rewarded by a varied and attractive walk.

THE WALK

From the car park **(1)** *turn left along a lane (West End) which leaves the A271 beside the Woolpack Inn. After 300 yards turn right along a gravel drive signed as a footpath. Where the drive ends, go over a stile, along a fenced path to a second stile and on in the same direction, down across a meadow to a third stile. Now, ignoring a stile on your right, fork left over a plank bridge and stile and climb across a field, aiming for a barn on the skyline. Go over a stile in an intermediate hedge and forward, passing to the left of a barn and on to join a lane where you must squeeze through a post and rail fence as there is no stile.*

Turn right and, almost immediately **(2),** *left through a gate. Skirt to the right of buildings, negotiating two more gates and drop downhill beside a high left-hand hedge. Continue in the same direction through a wood and gently up through an area of rough pasture to a stile beside a gate. Keep to the left edge of the field beyond, cross a footbridge in a wooded dip and climb across grass to find a stile to the right of a pond and to the left of a house at Studdens Farm. Go left along the gravel drive from the house to join the end of a lane* **(3).**

Bear right to follow this lane (Studdens Lane) northwards. After 500 yards, at a cross roads, turn left and at a road T-junction, go ahead over a stile beside a gate. Pass to the left of farm buildings, through more gates and follow the left edge of four successive fields. At the end of the fourth field, go ahead across a rough area for a few yards to join a farm access drive and turn right, following it as it passes to the left of the farm buildings at Clippenham Farm **(4).** *Beyond the buildings, go forward through a gate and then veer slightly left across a field to another gate providing access to a wood. Follow a clear path down through the wood where steps are cut into the bank as the gradient steepens. Cross a footbridge and stile to leave the wood, bear slightly left up across the next field, joining and following a right hand hedge for a few yards to a gateway. Cross the next field, this time veering very slightly right to find a stile and footbridge a few yards to the right of a prominent oak tree.*

A path continues along the left edge of a small vineyard. (If overgrown, a parallel alternative is possible between the first two rows of vines). At the edge of a garden, go left, passing to the left of a weather-boarded house (Batsford Barn). Join and bear right along the drive from the house, passing the larger, timber-fronted Batsford Farm House. After another 200 yards along the drive, where it bears right, fork left over a stile and head out across a field, aiming for a stile, in sight, at the far end, next to a power pole. Follow the right edge of the next field until, in the field corner, you can join a lane over a stile and turn left along it. When opposite the elegant red brick Iwood Place on the left **(5),** *turn right over a stile.*

You have been gradually gaining height since leaving Herstmonceux and are rewarded by a sweeping view eastwards across the Weald and southwards to the distant South Downs and even a glimpse of the sea to the east of Eastbourne.

Go forward along a left field edge, cross a gallop and drop down along the left edge of the field beyond. Towards the bottom of the hill, go forward along a track which crosses a culvert in a wooded dip. About 40 yards beyond the stream, fork right over or between wooden railings to follow a path through a wood, shortly with the high fence of a game bird enclosure on your right. Shortly, where this fence bends away to the right, downhill, go ahead along a path, indistinct in places, across a ditch and through the wood. After little more than 100 yards, bear right to leave the wood over a stile and head uphill to a gate which soon comes into sight at the right end of a block of woodland. Continue uphill with these trees, surrounding a large pond, to your left.

At the far corner of the wood, the right of way officially side steps to the left over a stile before resuming its original direction with the hedge to the right. At the time of writing this route was overgrown and difficult and you may find it easier to continue within the same field with the hedge on your left. Both routes rejoin at a gate after about 200 yards **(6).**

At this point, turn right and drop downhill beside a left hand post and rail fence with the farmhouse and nearby converted oast at Summertree Farm over to your left across a paddock. Where the fence on your left turns away to your left, carry on without change of direction, down across an undulating field to reach the bottom left field corner. Now go left over a stile built into a hunt jump and follow the right field edge with a wood on your right until you can go right over wooden rails. An overgrown path passes through a belt of woodland with a small pond to your right, Cross the eroded outflow from the pond with care and leave the wood over another hunt jump.

Batsford Farmhouse.

After a few yards, go forward over a stile and plank bridge and, immediately right, over a second stile and bridge. Cross a field, go through a gap next to a power pole and turn left along a left field edge. Pass between the buildings at Stonelands Farm, turn left to follow the concrete drive from the farm out to a lane and turn right. At the point where another lane goes off to the right **(7),** *turn left over a stile, cross a field to a second stile and continue in the same direction across the next field to a gate in the far right corner where you can join and go forward along a concrete track through a wooded dip and up to a stile beside a gate. Maintain direction up a bank and then veer slightly left across a field to another stile/gate combination, Carry on with a hedge on your right at first, go through a gap about 40 yards to the left of the field corner and cross the field beyond, veering very slightly left to find a stile in the next hedge, signed as a path diversion. Go forward along a right field edge to another stile and on along a concrete track with Hole Farm House on your right and a brick shed on your left* **(8).**

Follow the track until, opposite a pond on your right and a few yards short of a converted oast, you can turn left through a gate. The path ahead through waste ground doesn't look promising and may be overgrown with nettles. Things improve after a few yards where the path descends steps, crosses a newish footbridge and climbs through woodland, where you may have to dodge round fallen timber to reach a stile. Now climb steeply up a grassy slope, skirting to the right of a patch of gorse and to the left of a wood on the top of the hill. At the far end of this wood, go ahead over a stile and on with a hedge on your left and then along a grassy hedged track. Where the enclosed track ends, go ahead along a left field edge to a gate and out via the drive from a cottage to join a lane. Turn right and walk into Bodle Street Green.

At the road junction next to the White Horse Inn **(9),** *go ahead, signed to Herstmonceux and Windmill Hill. After about 350 yards, go right over a stile and left for a few yards to a second stile in the field corner. Now head diagonally out across the middle of a field, cross a stile in an intermediate fence, continue in the same direction down to a stile in a hedge and on over two more stiles in line ahead. A path then winds down through a wood. At a path junction, turn left, walking with a stream on your right until a footbridge takes you over the stream. Now bear half left across a field to a stile, in sight. Head squarely out across the field beyond to join and follow a fence along the right edge of two fields, passing under power lines immediately to the left of a pylon. Beyond a stile, veer slightly right across a field to find a hidden stile in the far right corner. Bear left passing to the right of the buildings at Nunningham Farm. Join the drive from the farm over a stile and bear right to follow it out via an estate road back into Herstmonceux opposite the Woolpack Inn.*

White Horse Inn, Bodle Street Green.